WINNING AT LOVE
It's More than Just Getting Lucky!

Copyright © 2014 Roger W. Breternitz CCht.
All rights reserved.

13-ISBN-978-0615922515
10-ISBN-0615922511

Library of Congress Control
Number: 2014908925

Cover - Logo Design & Publishing by Roger W. Breternitz CCht.
&

Laguna Niguel Ca.
www.awinnersway.com
www.vectorstudios.com

WINNING AT LOVE
It's more than just getting lucky!

Reprogram yourself to attract the "Right one" and recognize them when they come along

Winning comes from experience and experience comes from *PLAYING!*

GET IN THE GAME!

By Roger W. Breterntiz CCht.

FORWARD

It has been said that, "There's someone out there for everyone, if they can just find each other". Usually that phrase comes from someone who *thinks* they've got it "All together", while viewing someone else who (according to them) doesn't. So in an effort to make them feel better, more exalted, and important...they say, "I don't know how they found each other, but God bless'em. However, what is it that attracts two people? Is it looks, intellect, personality, what's the trigger that makes the heart flutter, the breathing increase, the face flushed and the knees weak? Some call it chemistry, but that's just what they say because they don't know what to call it, what IT is anyway is a mystery that we're still working on. The thought being that no matter how messed up and deranged person #1 is, there's someone out there, just as messed up, with the same level of derangement, inadequacies, and problems, who will view person #1 as someone who is just what they've been looking for. The trouble is, there are several parameters and factors that have got to be in place in order for this meeting to ever get to "First base". This book is all about most of those parameters, filters, and activators, that cause people to not only spend more than 2 minutes together in the first meeting, but have that second date/meeting, become intimate, move in together, get married, stay married, build a life together, and grow old together.

DEDICATION

Since I learned a lot about what love is and received a lot of it from my parents, I dedicate this book to my Mom & Dad. They provided a home filled with love, and guidance that gave me the internal blueprint for what love between two people should be. They were together for 47 years until their passing within two days of each other. So in their memory I say, "You did a great job Mom and Dad in helping implant the right belief systems in me."
I wish other people were this lucky, but that's who this book is for...the "Other" people.

Bless all of you out there who weren't as lucky as myself.

KEEP READING!

READ THIS!

AUTHOR'S NOTE:
It is a known fact that we remember less of what we READ, more of what we HEAR, more of what we SEE, and the retention goes up from there as we incorporate seeing AND hearing, then SEE, HEAR, and DOING.

It is for this reason that I have some paragraphs, concepts, and text or divisions within chapters repeated. The repetition is however not word for word, although it has much of the same information stated in different words, or additional explanations. This is in hopes of bringing about greater retention of information imparted, with the idea that if you *RETAIN* it you will *EMPLOY* it, which as you will find, is the definition of...

LEARNING: The *application* of knowledge acquired to ensure or change the end result of an endeavor or event.

IMPORTANT
I have also put some MARKER POINTS in several places to illustrate VERY important points in the book. When you see "**IMPORTANT**" think the words, "THIS IS WORTH THE PRICE OF THE BOOK" or "IF I LEARN ANYTHING FROM THIS BOOK, LEARN THIS!" These are things that very few people are aware of, and will give you a formidable edge in the singles meeting place. You would be good to highlight these sections or page mark them for reference.

JUST DO IT!

ACKNOWLEDGMENTS

Winning, it's a Lot More Fun
By
Roger W. Breternitz CCht.

NLP – The New Technology of Achievement
By
Steve Andreas & Charles Faulkner

The Law of Attraction
By
Esther & Jerry Hicks

Psycho-Cybernetics
By
Maxwell Malts

Formatting - Vector Studios

Table of contents

Chapter		Page
1	Who is this book for?	9
2	What actually is LOVE?	13
3	Love at first sight?	25
4	The Floppy Bird Story	35
5	Belief Systems	39
6	Changing **your** belief systems	47
7	The first 3 minutes	59
8	Prospecting (for that special person)	63
9	Non-verbal Cues	72
10	LUST at first sight	85
11	Confidence	91
12	Levels of attraction	98
13	Moth to a flame	103
14	First dates	111
15	Listening	119
16	First impressions	129
17	Sexual attraction	133
18	Getting lucky	143
19	Are you ready	153
20	Goal setting	163
21	Rejecting the "Wrong" person	175
22	Written in the stars	189
23	The "Kitty" syndrome	201
24	Value systems	205
25	Truth & Lies	211
26	Personality types	223
27	Dating in the modern world	239
28	Repelling the wrong person	253
29	How happy are you?	259
30	Putting it all together	275
31	Bonus section - Make your own cd	289

CHAPTER 1
WHO IS THIS BOOK FOR?

It's been said that there's no such thing as luck, good things come to you because you deserve it, you've worked for it, and you've made it happen. In life there are things that you do that will "Enhance" your chances of being or getting lucky in any area of your life, and love or attracting it is no different. Each day of your life you make a vast number of decisions, and the level, type, or amount of "Luck" you attract is a direct result of those decisions. When something happens to you for no apparent reason we call it luck, good or bad, there was no reason this should have happened, right?

NOT EXACTLY!

If you drive too fast in relation to the speed limit, go through red lights, cut people off, and are very aggressive behind the wheel, you're going attract negative things or "Bad luck", like a motorcycle cop with radar sitting where he "Shouldn't be" at that time of the day. So...don't leave your head on the chopping block after you throw an ax at your worst enemy. You would be attracting bad luck.

This book is about increasing your chances of

getting lucky in love, and not only attracting just that right person for only you, but repelling the wrong person as well. The part about repelling, that's just as important as the attracting, and very few people have achieved any level of skill at this, let alone mastered it, so hopefully you will learn the basics on which to build.

Just by the fact that you're reading this book means that it's for YOU, because of your desire to learn something new, bring about an event that will change your life, and bring you greater happiness, fulfillment, and joy. Which is, as you will learn about joy, is the best, greatest, and most fulfilling thing we can attract.

On the other hand, who else is it for? It's for the princess who feels she has kissed just about all the "Frogs" she is going to kiss, looking for Price Charming. She thinks he doesn't exist and instead of looking for Mr. Right, is looking for Mr. Right now!

It's for the young guy just out of high school who might not have been the captain of the football team, leader of the debate team or had his parents give him a new sports car for graduating with a C average. He knows he needs an "Edge", but is scared to go out on it.

It's for the couple in the Bob Seger song "Night moves", who are "Working on mysteries without any clues." Hopefully it will impart some of those clues to help prevent constant re-occurrences of stepping in the same "Bear traps" of love, attraction, and the bottomless pit of what seemed like a good idea at the time.

It's for the middle-aged guy who's lost a few hairs and gained a few pounds. He saw his reflection in a storefront window and was wondering who that fat guy was until he figured out it was him. He still wonders why the hottest girl in the bar won't talk to him, or buy him a drink. But then again he'll probably never think he needs this book, and continue doing what he's always done expecting different results with each attempt!

It's for the 50 year old Princess who's number of boyfriends are now in the double digits, but can't seem to find any that are "Good enough", so she'd rather spend time on the couch with a good book (hopefully this one).

It's for the Prince Charming that has it all together, and has a stable of starlet/model wannabe's, but just can't find one that can carry on a conversation without saying "Like" every third word and talk incessantly about her cat!

It's for just about anyone who wants to learn the power of attraction beyond looks, appearance, wealth, social standing, material possessions, and raw animal magnetism, even though they have all of that, or none of that going for them.

It's for the very few who have come to the realization that "Harmony" is the force that holds couples together after that first encounter. The mutual desire both have for the other one to achieve the best for their life. This harmony is the natural offset or "Side step" each one takes to allow the other person their own space to be themselves, while uplifting and contributing to their partner. Yes, even THAT person can benefit from this book.

So whoever you are, unless you've found your "One and only", which means you are going to be together for the rest of your life...you're still looking for that perfect person to fit their "Yin" with your "Yang"...this book is for you.

Good luck on your quest, as long as you *keep looking*, it *REALLY* increases your chances. When you give up looking for that person, it's like trying to win the Super Lotto without buying a ticket! **JUST DO IT!**

CHAPTER 2
WHAT ACTUALLY IS LOVE?

BEING IN LOVE

What is love anyway? There have been many definitions, thousands of philosophers have tried to define it, and we could go on and on trying to understand it forever, and never really come up with a true definition. If you get right down to it, Love is a state of mind, and a level of being. The kind of love that exists between two people is a oneness that makes each one care more about the other, and makes each one want the best for the other before themselves. How many people with a relationship like that would be arguing all the time?

HEART OVER MIND OR VISA VERSA

How many people have you known (or maybe you're one) who is so emotional that common sense goes out the back door when it comes to love, and relationships? These people are ruled by their heart, and even though they know what's best for them, they pick the emotional choice that causes them to end up getting hurt, and finally being thrown out the 10th story of that building called rejection. After they hit the pavement face first, they are helped up by someone who does the same thing to them when they thought they would never let it happen again!

They allow their heart to do their thinking for them instead of their simple common sense. On the other hand there are people who very rarely get hurt or have trouble in relationships because they are so sensible.

There once was a man who was in love with a very attractive woman who claimed to be in love with him. She made a high salary, was a very controlling, and very jealous type. It may have been because most of the men in her past cheated on her, lied to her or were less than truthful with her, and she was very defensive, even with him. She was always looking out the corner of her eye to catch him glancing at other women when it was almost impossible NOT to look at them, because of the way they were dressed, bent over, or some way that they made themselves stand out. He was, on the other hand not the jealous type and finally could not tolerate this behavior, and told her, "Look, I can't stand your jealousy and I'm out of here. I love you, but I'm not stupid, and I know we are never going to make it in the long run." His mind over ruled his heart, and made the choice that in the long run was the best thing for him, and her. He later found someone who was not jealous, was caring non-controlling, and they lived happily ever after. Like the song says, "You got to know when to hold 'em and know when to fold 'em".

"That's easy for you to say", you think. Sure it's always easy for a third party to stand outside the situation and give advice, but at some point in time you have to say, "Look…I'm watching my life go in a direction I don't like, and I've finally got to do something about it. It's time to start thinking with my brain instead of my heart (or other portions of my anatomy) or I will keep getting the same results each time I am put in the same situation". The amazing part is, when you DO accomplish thinking with your common sense, just once, it becomes easier the next time, and the next time, until you are finally in control (more than before) of your life as far as relationships. Then this little victory filters over into other parts of your life as it relates to you gaining more control over the way you wish things would be going in general. You put all this together and it's called GROWTH. Some people learn from their mistakes, and this is also called growth, some people just keep plodding along and never learn, even though they keep getting the same results each time. The funny thing is, that they say the same thing each time they get "Stomped on" or step in a relationship bear trap..."Why didn't I listen to myself", or "Why didn't I see this coming". The truth is, they DID see it coming, but chose not to listen or not to see, because this time they thought, "It will be different".

WHY YOU LIKE SOMEONE

WOMEN: What attracts you to someone, is it looks, the car they drive, the high paying job they have, the house they live in, or their lifestyle?

All of the above come under a heading of "What can you DO for me?

LOOKS: Naturally women are attracted to a guy because he's tall, dark and handsome as the saying goes. It's the part of being human, and the thing that activates the response we call EMOTION! Many times this overshadows every other flaw in his character UNTIL those flaws make you realize it's not worth it. Hopefully you haven't walked down the isle of matrimony, have children in college, a summer home by the lake, and belong to the country club. If do have those things, you were REALLY good at overlooking those faults, and capitalized on that phrase, "What can you DO for me?"

HIS CAR: It gives you lots of excitement, it's exhilarating, just plain FUN! It gets old quickly.

HIS PROFESSION: He's a doctor, lawyer, CEO, and makes a high salary. It means security for you and all the stuff above. What can you do for me?

HIS HOUSE: Means security, level of comfort, status when it's big, and expensive. What can it DO for me.

HIS LIFESTYLE: He is international, takes you

along on exotic trips, vacations, and get-aways. It's exciting and fun. What can you DO for me?

MATERIAL STUFF: I knew this guy (not high on the scale of physical attractiveness) who related to me his conversation with this girl he was wanted to marry. He was financially well off, had a couple of houses, one in a resort area etc., and had an upper level lifestyle. He asked her, "So what would it take to close the deal (get married)?" Without skipping a beat she said,"4 carats". The ring set him back $17,000. 6 months later she broke it off! What can you do for me?

MEN:

LOOKS...Yes this is probably the most important factor for men, because it is a projection of their accomplishments. Some of these accomplishments are the *ability* to attract someone who would be considered a "Hottie". Some of his *abilities* would be, his level of handsomeness. If he was considered handsome he could NEVER be seen without "Arm candy" portraying a like level of *his* attractiveness. What can she DO for me?

If they're not jaw dropping good looking, then

it (being seen with a hottie) means they may make a ton of money, and have all the stuff mentioned in the paragraphs above, and people will think, "Well, he must have SOMETHING going for him?" THAT'S What can she DO for me, provide a place to display my wealth.

All of the above illustrations come under the "What can you DO for me", category, and it is a recipe for relationship disaster, UNLESS there is truth, honesty, love, and mutual harmony above it all. Because, when you take away all that material "Stuff"...and it WILL eventually be gone, what is left? If you are both still together, that's it, that's all it comes down to, having each other.

The purpose of this book is to give you a road map to steer you through a maze of distractions, and pitfalls, guiding you to a destination you have set for yourself. That destination SHOULD BE to find somebody that cares about you as much as you care about them, and *their* happiness. All this other stuff is just icing on the cake.

To increase your success in relationships it

helps to first of all, LEARN what kind of person is NOT the right one for you and your life, and RECOGNIZE this person a mile off. Many times it's easier to know what you DON'T want instead of what you do want. You would be surprised how many people actually have no idea what they want in a mate, lover, or companion. They just go floating down the river of life like a boat without a rudder or any oars, allowing themselves to be pushed wherever the flow takes them. For that person you've got to say that they deserve what they get. The phrase "Action begets results" is more powerful than you think. If you want something to happen, you have to take action to at least TRY to make it happen. It's really difficult to win the lottery when you don't buy a ticket. Yet some people keep saying "When I win the lottery I will……..." yet they forget to buy a ticket, or just don't get around to it, and this behavior is repeated over and over again. Once again, it's *action;* bodies at rest tend to stay at rest. If you take the slightest little action, it keeps you from being at rest, and gets you going just a little, then it's easier to take bigger steps toward your goal. Accomplishing a goal, any goal even a small one, gives you self-confidence, and nothing attracts the opposite sex (or people in general) better than self-confidence.

When it comes to men and women relationships, there are still untold masses that no matter how old they are, they're still "Working on mysteries without any clues". Someone once said, "Learning is the APPLACTION of knowledge acquired".

You haven't LEARNED your lesson, unless you APPLY the knowledge you acquire from your mistakes to keep you from making the same mistakes again...and again!

To become successful at forming relationships the trick is not only recognizing that the person you are with is NOT the person you are looking for, but also how FAST you can recognize this. Some people only recognize this AFTER they get married, some after they get engaged, some do after the first 6 months, and when you get it down to less that a couple of months...then, you are making progress, you've learned a few lessons. Some people are really good and can make a pretty accurate decision after the first date. THIS is where you want to be, when you start thinking with your brain instead of your heart.

SEE CHAPTER ON "REPELLING THE WRONG PERSON"

There are a host of Internet sites that take a wealth of information from you to hopefully match you up with someone who will be "Perfect" for you, someone with which you'll live happily ever after.

They try to find out what you like, don't like, religious preference, smoke, don't smoke, and a host of other questions that you didn't even know were questions until you paid the money to join their "Thing".

They take all the information, boil it down, convert it into zeros, and ones, put it in a computer and come up with your perfect match...or so they think. There is a little factor that is never considered in this foolproof equation, and that's the "Human factor". There is just something about a person's mind, personality, needs and wants that seems to escape the fastest most powerful computer no matter how much data is submitted. This human factor cannot be included, cannot be second guessed, and nobody can put their finger on exactly what is going to make both parties attracted to each other, until it actually happens.

If it were easy everybody would be married to just the right person, living in total harmony, there would be no divorce, everyone would have a 50th wedding anniversary, and the world would be a wonderful place. But what happened to the perfect match? It seemed perfect at the time. Those are the "Game changing" words, perfect **at the time.** Time changes everything, and it changes people most of all. You are not the person you were a year ago, 5 years ago and certainly not 10 years ago. With that said, we can realize if there is so much change going on between couples it's easy to understand how they can develop into personalities that begin to repel each other instead of attract each other.

Little things become big things when they keep happening over and over and you don't want them to happen even twice. People become less tolerant of objectionable behavior, and less forgiving. So what IS the most powerful thing that holds two people together, what's the "Glue" in their relationship? It's what this book is all about...

LOVE! And that's caring for someone when they don't deserve that care. Helping someone that doesn't want help or admit that they need help. NOT pointing out someone's faults when you could. And in the end, giving of your time and efforts to someone who doesn't appreciate your gift immediately.

Winning at love is the most difficult accomplishment to achieve, because you don't have total control over the entire situation, and "Trying" hard doesn't improve your chances of winning. It's the only game where "Giving in" gets you closer to the goal line of "Winning".

Winning someone's heart, trust, and love in return. Don't think about it...

JUST DO IT

CHAPTER 3
LOVE AT FIRST SIGHT

Everyone has heard the term "Love at first sight", and most everyone has had that experience in some way. Love in this case would be an attraction so powerful you can't think of anything else, see anything else, perceive anything else, and you are blind to all other things outside of this one focus of your perception. A high degree of physical beauty does this to people, and gives them this "Tunnel vision" they are experiencing with the subject of their focus, or in some cases MIS-focus.

Let's look at the value earlier mentioned, which was "High degree of beauty". It doesn't actually have to be a member of the opposite sex, it can also be something that, in the viewer's eyes, captures their attention, admiration, and full attention.

It could be a $100,000 sports car, a $15,000 shotgun, a million dollar sport fishing yacht, or anything that this particular viewer puts at the top of their list of sought after items.

In all of the above cases the love at first sight phenomena never really takes root unless there is the POSSIBILITY of the viewer actually acquiring, or being successful with the object of their infatuation. For example, if they see a $100,000 sports car, but only have a 4-door family sedan budget, their arousal would not be even close to that of the millionaire who could afford $150k for that car, and sees it on sale for $100k. There has to be a close proximity of the object of desire to the possibility of acquisition.

More simply put, if there is no chance of a successful end result meeting, use or implementation of this person, place or thing, it is most likely dismissed without continued attraction. Examples would be, the guy who's working as a fry cook, driving a 15 year old Junker, sees a new $200,000 Bentley and doesn't immediately think to himself, "I just GOTT'A have that car, what can I do to get that car?!"

By the same token, an out of shape, 55 year old bald guy with the polyester suit and cigarette dangling out of the corner of his mouth, doesn't think he's got a chance with the hottie, part time aerobics instructor at the corner of the bar that looks like Miss USA…or maybe he does! But that's another whole set of uncontrolled variables we'll go into later.

Love at first sight is a very unpredictable thing that very rarely happens between to people, and is the result of just the right variables coming together at just the right time under just the right conditions. The trouble is, it is not usually a mutual experience for BOTH people, because both people are usually at different places, levels, and or positions in their lives. In most meetings between two people, the "Elephant in the room" is always the thought of "What do you bring to the table". If it's "Well I brought filet mignon, and you brought a burger", now we have a miss-match.

In more simpler terms there are several areas of what you actually do bring to that table called the

"SMORGASBOARD OF LIFE"

WOMEN RELATED

1. SECURITY: (Women) This is more important for women, because a woman is usually the

sub-dominant one in the relationship, the non-bread winner, the weaker sex, and we could go on about that for ever, but…how secure a future could a man provide for her in this instance? Within this category we have several sub-categories:

a) VOCATION: Who would provide more security, a doctor, lawyer, professional man or a blue collar worker, bus boy, day laborer etc.? This is possibly the reason you see many "Miss-matches" between couples, An example would be, the trophy wife, plain looking husband. She is willing to trade physical attractiveness for security, and he can provide this. An elderly Aunt of mine (Aunt Hattie) once said to a young girl, *"Never marry for money sweetheart, but let love go where money is!"*

There are loads of examples of how this phenomena has NOT worked well for people, and there have been songs written about it. Take for instance the song by the Eagles, "Lying Eyes", about a girl who trades being with someone she really loves for an old man to take care of her. It never ends well.

b) PHYSICAL POWER: In providing physical security, which would be better, a 6' 4" 265lb. in shape Karate expert, or 125lb. pencil neck geek type of computer nerd? A woman thinks of these things in the back of her mind first of all and eventually it comes to the front of her mind if things get more intimate or "Chummy".

2. ADACEDEMIC BACKGROUND: Does this person have a college degree and if so what level, a Bachelors, Masters, or PhD? It's all about levels of achievement in what you bring to this table that most times even gains you admittance to the "Dinning room." In the Mensa club, you have to have an IQ in the upper 2% of the general population to even be admitted.

It's easy to understand why someone who has achieved a high level of academic accomplishment would be *repulsed* by someone who used profanity and improper English. Very simply, they are on two different levels of awareness, income, and general existence. One is willing to do just about anything to become attractive to the other one, but doesn't have the "Right stuff". Even the "Country boy" knows, you don't go hunting bear with a slingshot!

LOOKS: Level of attractiveness is a very illusive thing to try and measure, because what is super attractive to one person may be just average to someone else. Everyone has different "Turn on's and turn off's", and some of the "Turn on's" may be so strong as to blot out all the other negatives about that person.

CUTE METERS

There are no "Cute meters" or "Beauty scopes" out there that you can just hold up to someone and WHANG…a needle jumps across a dial stopping at a number, and now you have a value you can assign to them for the rest of their life. However; we all do actually have a "cute meter" imbedded in our brain, our DNA, our biological make up. This is called our belief system, and it tells us what we deserve, how much we can accomplish in life, and in this instance the level of "Cute" we can attract in another potential mate. This has probably been created by our personal history. Over the years because of the level of "Cute" in members of the opposite sex we have been able to attract as

"Intimate" friends or acquaintances, we have *acquired* a rating system of how good looking a guy/girl we can attract, which in turn has given us a self-rating level. We have been on a date with many different guys/girls and some are MUCH better looking than others. The "Best" looking guy/girl we've ever had a relationship with has set a standard for us to believe that's the highest level of looks we can achieve. So what happens when Mr/Ms Wonderful, Mr/Ms "Better than we've ever had", comes along? Some people get tongue tied, Ga Ga, falling down drunk with infatuation, and will overlook ANY discrepancy, any type of fault, or negative mannerism. It's called being "Star struck".

SENARIO: While in 5th grade, 10 year old Larry likes Sally, she's the most adorable, cutest thing in the class and Larry asks her if he can walk her home. She says "No" and walks home with Billy, who is over the top on the scale of handsome. He can't figure out why, after all, he asked her first.

Betty, who is not the cutest thing in class, asks Larry if he would walk *HER* home. He's still thinking of Sally and says NO. Both Betty and Larry have had their first experience of belief system anchoring.

FAST FORWARD 5 YEARS: Larry is 15, and a freshman in high school at the first Homecoming dance and seeks out Sally, the Homecoming Queen, asks her to dance, she gives him that "Don't you ever learn" look, goes over and grabs Billy, who is now the football quarter back, they dance, and leave together. Betty comes up and says, "Hey Larry, let's dance", and he thinks "Why not." This is known as a "Re-augmentation" of a value belief system.

Sally, Billy, Larry, and Betty have just further anchored a belief system of "Cuteness value" and potential accomplishment that will be with them for the rest of their lives, getting stronger every time the same thing happens. And it probably will, many times over.

15 years later at the class reunion: Larry has become a successful investment broker and pulls up in a $100,000 Ferrari; Sally asks Larry if he'd like to have a night cap at her place. What's

the moral of this story?

TRUTH: MONEY TRUMPS LOOKS EVERY TIME. But we'll get into that later. (See: Floppy Bird Story Next). So in this "Love at first sight" scenario there has to be a "Plausible" level of attraction between two people with each of them being on somewhat of the same plato of life, bringing equal "Things" to that Smorgasbord of Life table.

SYMBIOTIC RELATIONSHIPS

So what exactly is a symbiotic relationship anyway? Simply put it is an unlikely relationship where each party (although seemingly miss-matched) is providing something that the other party wants, needs, and can't get anywhere else, in return for receiving a like thing or service that can't be gotten anywhere else. Like the little bird (Egyptian Plover) that picks the pieces of leftovers from the Crocodile's teeth so it doesn't decompose and cause the Croc pain. The 'Croc being extremely grateful, refrains from chomping down and eating the bird.

So, next time you see two people who seem

miss-matched, don't burst a brain cell trying to figure out what the symbiotic relationship is between them. Just be happy for both of them, write it on your "Mental clipboard" of interesting data, and go on with your search for that perfect match.

CHAPTER 4

THE FLOPPY BIRD STORY

Once upon a time there was a remote island, on which a unique species of bird lived and flourished. These birds were called "Floppies". They were very distinctive in their marking because no two were alike. Some were very beautiful with gorgeous reflective coloring in their feathers, and different patterns caused by this intricate coloring. Some were not as beautiful as others, and no two, male or female were exactly alike.

The got their name because of the strange mating dance they performed and only mated for one season with the same bird of the opposite sex. The next season they chose a different partner to court, and maybe or maybe not become successful at mating. The dance they performed was called "Flip-Flopping", (nothing to do with political candidates) and consisted of one of the birds (male or female) doing the dance for the other, usually the lesser attractive one doing the "Flip-Flop" dance for the more attractive one. The actual dance consisted of the bird lying on its stomach or back and flopping over on it's reverse side, and then repeating the act as many times as it felt necessary to gain the affection of the other bird. Herein lies the point of the story. The prettier or better looking the "Dance-EE"…or watcher, happened to be, the more and higher "Flip-Flops" the "Dancer" felt it was necessary to do in order to gain the affection of, and be able to mate with that particular bird. If the degree of "Good looking-ness" between the two was a vast difference then there were a lot more "Flip-Flops" to be done to make the watcher "Like" or be attracted to the dancer. Sometimes if there was too great a difference in looks the watcher would actually turn away from the dancer signaling he or she was not even interested and the dance was terminated.

Sometimes the dancer would not take "NO" for an answer and kept doing the dance which had an even more negative effect on the sought after partner, and that watcher would fly away in an attempt to get away from the suitor. This enraged the suitor so badly that it would attempt to catch the other bird and was so mad it could not see clearly, and would fly into a tree or rock cliff.

The important thing to take note of, was that the amount of "Flip-Flops" done by one bird were in direct correlation to the difference of attractiveness or degree of beauty in the two birds. There were very few extremely pretty or strikingly colored birds on the island and when one like this courted the other, very few "Flip-Flops" were performed. It seemed like both knew that they were mutually attracted to each other and very few "Flip-Flops" were done. Once in a great while a more brightly colored bird would be the dancer, and in this case would have to do hardly more than one "Flip-Flop" to gain the approval of the lesser bird.

Does it sound like a singles bar? The question is, how many "Flip-Flops" will you do for that person that who is the object of your affection? Some people will go to great lengths to attract someone prettier or much better looking than they, therein lies the problem, and that is where the "Game-playing" starts. What is the basis on which you make your decision to take a partner in a relationship or marriage? Is it looks, money, social position, possession, or because you both just get along?

Only you can answer these questions, but you already have a pretty good idea of what the answers are. The question is, do you *believe* the answers in the back of your mind that are straining to get to the front, or are you afraid to acknowledge they even exist? Nobody knows the person you really are except you, when no one's around but you. Start accepting those answers...*THEY'RE REAL!*

So get real, and step up to the bar of honesty, throw fantasy in the wastebasket, and start living for real. It really IS better on THAT side of the fence! When you're being yourself, and that isn't enough for someone, you don't need them anyway!

CHAPTER 5

BELIEF SYSTEMS

Psychologists have written books on this, behavior modification gurus have held endless seminars on it, and they all come up with basically the same general idea. Your belief system is what gives you the idea you CAN do something, MAY be able to accomplish something, or WILL be successful at completing the goal you have set for yourself. The opposite is also true. It doesn't matter if you think you can do something or you can't, one thing is sure...YOU'RE RIGHT!

So what actually is a belief system, how do you get it, and how do you change it if it's not giving you the desired end result you want in your life?

WHAT IT IS

A belief system is what your INNER mind believes about any one of hundreds of events that you have experienced, or think you WILL experience in the future. It is anticipating the positive or the negative occurrences that might be a result of your past actions together with your immediate reactions that could "Possibly" result in your future success or failure in immediate or long term future events. Basically it boils down to WHAT YOU REALLY BELIEVE, and this, many times is not what you THINK you believe. Everyone thinks they believe all kinds of positive things about themselves, that they are basically a good person, they like puppies and children, they give donations to the less fortunate, and deserve the best life has to offer for them. NOT! That is what their CONSCIOUS mind *thinks* they think. However, some of their past behavior suggests this is all fabrication, because their actual actions and *reactions* do not support the existence this belief system.

TRUTH OF THE MIND: *THE WAY YOU PRECEIVE YOURSELF IS ONE THING, WHAT YOU DO (YOUR ACTIONS)EITHER SUPPORTS AND RENFORCES THAT BELIEF, OR WEAKENS THAT BELIEF, AND SUPPORTS THE OPPOSITE OF THAT BELIEF.*

POWER OF PERSONAL HISTORY

The problem is: We are not God. We are human and we make mistakes in our quest (if you have one) to better ourselves, to upgrade our existence to a higher level of love and happiness, and many times we make "Bad" choices that create a less than positive personal history. This personal history is 10 times more powerful at shaping our belief systems than our conscious efforts or thoughts to make significant changes in our outward behavior that will materialize our goal whatever that goal is. Therefore there is a gap in our reality concerning the event/s that we actually experience as opposed to what we THINK we should experience because of who we THINK we are, and the abilities we THINK we posses.

A golfer hits a beautiful drive 300 yards down the middle of the fairway...ONCE. That person thinks they're Arnold Palmer, they think they should "Go Pro". The trouble is, their actual SCORE tells a different story, and even though their actual score is a glaring sign flashing in red YOU'RE AN AMATURE...they still believe they should be in the hall of fame. They have a

"Skewed view" of reality, but their personal history (their SCORE) tells an entirely different story. This personal history brings their TRUE belief system down to reality, and they hit the next 3 drives into the rough.

They only remember the "Good" parts of their personal history, but the score card brings, or *should* bring them back to reality. Even then some people refuse to see that reality.

STORY

There once was a boy in high school who was a good athlete, marginal good looks, his body is in great physical shape, and he's a star on the football field. He enjoys a lifestyle of a popular person all the time he's in high school. He has a personal history of being the "Big dog" in his environment or as they say, "A big fish in a small pond." Because of this he doesn't have to "Try" very hard to get whatever he wanted from life as he knows it. His grades are marginal because the school wants him on the football team and his teachers give him some slack with elevating his grades, and of course all the best looking cheerleaders want to date him. Because of his athletic ability he gets a 1 year scholarship in football from a state university. His "Pond" just got a little bit bigger. Now he is up against a higher level of competition, but he still has the same belief system caused by his personal history from high school. He thinks he should be as successful in this new environment as he was in high school but this reality is about to change. The players are bigger, hit harder, and the "Tricks" he used before to make touchdowns don't work on these guys. His belief system says "I'm a champion" but the statistics tell a different story. His recent personal history (the actual stats) say he is a sub-performer, but all he can remember is the way he "Use to" win games.

The competition for female attention is much more demanding because the women are more sophisticated in what they want in a man, and there are many more men to choose from. Many of the guys are better looking than our high school "Star", have a hot car, not to mention a better future as a doctor, lawyer, or professional man. Suddenly he gets his first lesson in "Life reality". There is a song by Paul Simon, called "One man's ceiling is another man's floor", which means, no matter where you are in life, there's always someone above you in many areas of proficiency. Unless you are #1 in the world at your sport, corporate level, or the president of the United States...there's always someone who's your "Boss" as far as being better, smarter, prettier, more handsome, or more intelligent than you in your chosen field. Your success in life just depends on how you want to handle it.

The reason we are talking about belief systems here is because, in the search for that special person, or that perfect mate, you are always being either consciously or subconsciously evaluated by your own inner mind as to what you THINK you deserve as far as this mythical "Perfect" person. When someone comes along that is "Too good" for you according to your belief system, or "Out of your league" in your estimation, you begin to say and do things to cause that person to be looking at their watch, have to "Go to the restroom" and in essence drive them away from you. This happens even though you are seriously attracted to them, like them very much, and think they could be your "One and only". It's very simple, your belief system says you don't deserve someone that good looking, that smart, that successful or that "Perfect" for you, and you find a way to let them slip through your fingers.

So how do you change this belief system to attract instead of repel the special person you're looking for?

That is what this book is all about, changing that belief system to make you a winner at love, or at least attracting a higher level of person into your life, than you now think you can attract.

TRUTH AXIOM: *It doesn't matter if you think you will fail or succeed at something, one thing is true, most of the time, you'll always be right!*

CHAPTER 6

CHANGING *YOUR* BLEIEF SYSTEM

There is a saying about humility, "If you know you have it, you don't have it". The same thing goes for the subconscious mind, which is the creator of all your belief systems. If you know (or are aware) that you are consciously trying to make an effort to change your beliefs about yourself, then you are making a <u>conscious</u> effort, which has *very little* success in the end result. That end result is of course…CHANGE. An example is, this guy/girl knows they need to loose 25 pounds to be able to attract the kind of person they want to have as a boyfriend/girlfriend, lover, mate etc. They say to themselves over and over again how they need to drop the weight, but still keep eating like hungry wolf. No matter how hard they try to curb their over eating habit they keep doing the same thing while at the same time saying how they need to change. Their INSIDE belief system is telling them to eat to satisfy a need they have manufactured, even though their conscious efforts are to eat less, work out more and be more active. The INSIDE voice, or belief

ALWAYS wins out.

RULE OF CHANGE: *Change the inside first and the outside changes automatically.*

The most effective way of changing your inner or subconscious beliefs is to do it through mental reprogramming techniques such as hypnosis, mental visualization, and or relaxation reprogramming therapy. This brings about a more permanent change in what you really think about yourself, your abilities, and what you deserve. The second you adopt a new belief system as your existing reality, things begin to change toward the direction in which you believe. However it's pretty hard to believe you are a successful, attractive person when you're 30 pounds over weight and your clothes look like you just stepped out of a time machine from the 70s. There is this little thing called the "Mirror of reality", or in some cases just a plain mirror, which you would think in some people's houses, does not exist at all.

If you follow the rule of attraction, "You attract what you are yourself", and you expect to attract a higher level (better looking, prettier, smarter, more educated, successful) person, then you've got to BECOME a higher level person yourself. You have two choices:

1. You can stay the way you are, if you're happy with that, then you will have to be happy with the person you are going to attract. They are going to look like, act like and talk like you. If you don't like that kind of a person then don't EXPECT someone better than you to be attracted to you in your present state.

2. You can begin to realize where you need to improve, set some short term, attainable goals and work toward them. You can't change yourself into Prince/Princess Charming over night, but you CAN change your determination to do so overnight. This would be that first step in that "Teflon coated" principal that we are now calling CHANGE! It is very slippery, hard to hold on to, and seems to get away from us just when we think we've got it nailed down.

Once again, this involves that word called...CHANGE. How much change is involved depends upon how far away you presently are from the level and type of person you want to attract. Following the rule of attraction, if you're the worst LOOKING guy in the place (over weight, poorly groomed/dressed and had to use the bus to get there) you can't attract the best looking girl in the place, who pulls in driving a Bentley. Since each journey begins with the first step, take a good look at yourself both physically and mentally. Don't sugar coat what you see. The more truthful you allow yourself to be WITH yourself, the quicker you can begin to devise a plan for taking that first step on the new journey called CHANGE!

Behavior Modification

(Real change)

When people talk about change in their lives, they usually do it when they are "Walking the plank" of life over deep shark infested waters and there's nowhere else to go. Why, because people always follow the path of least resistance like a river flowing down a mountain. As long as they have their 54 inch Blue Ray TV with 800 channels, along with their Lazy Boy chair and favorite beverage after a meal that would feed the Ugandan population for a week…they are happy, so why change? Then the doctor comes along and when he's checking their heart beat with a stethoscope says…Hum-mmm. Which is not what you want to hear from your doctor when he's checking your heartbeat with a stethoscope. He then tells you, your heart is not beating correctly and you need to lose some weight because you're too FAT! Which is what he told you the last time you were in to see him, only this time it's not a request, it's an order, with a time limit. Hence the plank over shark infested waters gets shorter. You need to CHANGE.

Your boss tells you that your efforts are not up to "Par", and he's not talking about your golf game either. You didn't "Make quota" last month, and now you have to come in on the weekends to make it up, or go look for another job, which is known as a threat to your "Survival mechanism" and now you have to start actually WORKING, or as we say, CHANGE. All because of the economy, and people not buying your "Stuff" like they did before, and so you need to change what you do, how you do it, and how often you do it, and it's all very unsettling, because we DO NOT LIKE that word…CHANGE!

When people try to make a change to their behavior, it's mostly what we call "Overt" behavioral change, which means it's a change on the surface, but down inside the inner mind of the old behavior pattern still exists, and it will, given time, worm it's way back to the surface. Then that person will soon begin to revert back to the "Old Man", or woman, that they were before setting out on that wonderful adventure they thought they were embarking on, called, CHANGE. They always ask themselves the question, "Why didn't it work, why can't I change my behavior, why do I always revert back to that person I don't like under certain circumstances?" Why, people have been asking that question for hundreds of years, and have struggled with unsuccessful results for just as long.

The mind is a mystery to any of those who study it, and becomes more of a mystery the longer we study it. However; one thing has become apparent to psychologists and other "Mental experts". *Conscious* efforts to make changes are the least effective in behavior modification attempts, because the desired changes never get permanently communicated to the deeper, inner mind, the SUB-conscious mind. This controls all our outward behavior, and is the robot, so to speak, that controls that behavior. Reprogram the "Robot", and the outward behavior changes quickly.

So, how do you RE-program this Robot? That's what has made people like Tony Robbins, Richard Bandler (NLP), and a host of other psychological "Gurus" tons of money. It is the ACT of reprogramming the subconscious to deliver the outward behavioral changes that we are seeking. THIS is why these people get the money they command, to SHOW you how to accomplish this reprogramming.

If it were easy we'd all be living in the house we wanted, driving a "Rolls", married to just the right person, our kids would all grow up to be successful "Whatever's", and the world would be a wonderful place. So why is that not the case for everyone of us, or 50% of us, or 10% of us or even 1% of the population? Because, it is the BELIEF SYSTEM that we have in place. Once again this is the SUB-CONSCIOUS belief system we're talking about here. The belief system you can't change by telling yourself (consciously) over and over again that you want to change. This is going to require a LOT of work on your part.

Part 1: Learn self-Hypnosis (covered later) it's not that difficult.

This is the most "Belief changing" tool you will ever possess! It is first the act of learning how to reprogram your mind to get you the results you want. The first rule for change is " Change the inside first and the outside changes automatically, and quickly". Buy some hypnosis CDs on the subject at which you want to become better. If it's quitting smoking or losing weight, there are pages of web sites dedicated to this. One is http://www.awinnersway.com it has over 20 subjects that a person would want to improve themselves in many different areas of life. Some people want to be able to get over the hurdle of feeling like they DESERVE to win at their favorite sport. They always find a way to tank the match, or lose the tournament at the last minute or 11th hour, because they get too nervous, or can't concentrate well enough under the pressure of WINNING, not losing, but winning. The fear of winning is a subject that would fill another complete book.

Part 2: Let it happen

Once you have your programming in place, don't try to second guess it, change it at the last minute, remake the input, just let it happen the way it was meant to when you do your best. The more things work out, the more things WILL work out, again and again. Success begets success, the best time to make a sale, is just after you've MADE a sale, and so on and so on.

Change is never easy, because this is the most uncomfortable thing that happens to us in all of our lives. We like the way things are, but are not satisfied with the way things are...right? "Things", could be better, they could always be "Better". Even Hugh Heffner thinks things could be better, and look at his life. As a matter of fact, do look at his life. It wasn't always high living, beautiful women, houses, and cars. He put a lot of money, effort, and sacrifice into the fist issue of Playboy, not knowing if any of it would be received, or squelched by the readers, and of course the sensors! He took a chance, but it was a chance. He didn't sit back and say, "What if it doesn't work, I'll lose all the initial capital, I'll be broke and on the street, I'll be a loser, people will scorn me etc.". No, he just did it. His belief system was that of a winner, "How can it fail" attitude, and look what happened. He may not be the richest man in the world, but is probably the most coveted man in the world. Who would not want to trade place with Hugh Heffner? Because he just DID IT.

So, if you want change in your life, don't wait for a "Reason" to do it, don't wait until the "Time is right" to do it, because the time will never be right, and the right reason will never come...just DO IT, and worry about the consequences later. Keep trying, keep the effort for change foremost in your mind, because what you think about most is what you end up getting, even if it's not good for you! So, if you think only about the good, and positive aspects of your goal, that is what you will attract in our "Attraction Universe". Never forget the phrase, "Thoughts are things", they WILL become reality if you think them enough, so stay positive in those thoughts! We live in an "Attraction Universe", which means you attract what you think about most, and it doesn't matter if you believe that or not, it is still one of the laws of our Universe. So in the reprogramming of your inner mind if you think about what you need, and will enjoy when you get it, you will attract that thing or things to you like a magnet.

How does reprogramming work?

Reprogramming the inner mind, or inner belief system is a simple method of replacing one habit with another. You cannot change a habit, like smoking for instance. You have to REPLACE it with another habit, it is like forcing one bad habit out of our existence by forcing another good habit in it's place. That's why it's called RE-programming. The trouble is, you can't do it on a conscious level, because the inner mind which controls all behavior is on the

SUB-conscious level, and you can try to change on a conscious level until you are "Blue in the face", but permanent change will never happen. It will never become a reality, because the root of the problem still exists. It's like cutting down a lemon tree and leaving the stump. Pretty soon new growth sprouts from the stump and you expect it to bare…apples?

You need to create your own behavior modification system, by thought materialization, or creating a recording on a tape or CD that constantly tells you the affirmations you need to hear while you are in a deeper state of relaxation or even sleep.

Check the sections of this book for writing a reprogramming script to read into a tape recorder or CD burner and begin to change your inner belief system to bring you toward a lasting and permanent change for the better. Remember, nothing is as easy, or as hard as it looks, the <u>2nd time you look at it.</u> So…JUST DO IT.

CHAPTER 7

THE FIRST THREE MINUTES

This could be the most important information you will ever receive as far a how to influence people, attract or repel someone, and in general make a good or bad, first impression. They say that you never get a second chance to make a first impression. So this deals with making that first impression, and it is done in the first three minutes of interaction. Talk, talk, talk, that's what everyone wants to do when they first meet someone. They want to talk about themselves, and their accomplishments, in hopes the other person, or the object of their affection…or potential affection, hears all this verbiage and is somehow impressed with how great they are, or how great they SAY they are.

CONVERSATION

One time I thought I was doing a friend of mine a favor and set him up with a blind date with this girl. She was cute, and out-going (more on the out-going than I realized). I thought they would get along fairly well. The next time I saw him at work, I asked how it went. I could see he was trying to temper his response considerably, when he said, "Whoa, this chick must have had too much coffee, or power drink or something, 'cause I couldn't get a word in edgewise, does she ever shut up?" I had just moved into this large apartment complex, I didn't know very many people at the time but as the years went buy I became friends with a small group of tenants and to all of us, this girl became known as "Chatty Kathy". She never learned the art of listening and was very difficult to be around for more than 5 minutes, because of this constant stream of speech that endlessly flowed from her mouth.

If you want to make a positive FIRST impression on someone, listen more than you talk, ask more questions about the other person, and *remember* the answers.

NAME CALLING

While we are talking about remembering something, here's a great tip. If you want to make a positive impression on someone, REMEMBER their name! How many times have you heard someone say, "I'm sorry, what was your name, I'm so bad with names." Of course they're bad with names, they SAY they're bad with names, that is their belief system talking and reinforcing the fact that they're bad with names. When you hear someone tell you their name, repeat it over and over and over again in your mind, to yourself. Keep saying it to yourself, use it in a "Made up" sentence to yourself if you have to. Just do it. Then, after a while in the conversation when you slip their name into a sentence, their "Affinity level" for you will be at a new high. When it's time to part company and you use their name when saying goodbye, they WILL remember you over all the other people who are, "Bad with names". This is a major factor in being able to win friends and influence people of any gender. Each and every minute, especially in the first three minutes, you are making an impression on them. Once that impression is made it's hard to change, hence the statement, "You never get a second chance to make a first impression".

Remembering someone's name and using it in the interaction with them in the first three minutes is just about the most powerful way to burn a very positive impression into their conscious mind. The problem most people have with this aspect of interaction is "Remembering" to remember to do it. So, in your effort to excel at remembering someone's name, set yourself a goal at the beginning of the day, that says, "Today I WILL remember the name of the first new person I meet." When you meet someone "New" even before they tell you their name, you will be ready to receive and remember this information easily.

CHAPTER 8

PROSPECTING

(For that Special Person)

You have two schools of thought when trying to find a person who fits your "Wish list", or just has a few of the qualifications you're looking for in someone.

APPROACH #1: You are LOOKING for them.

Wow! What a revelation you're thinking. "So you mean I just go out with the **intention** of stumbling across my one and only"? Not "Just" go out and run into them, but consider…then enact the exact behavior that will increase the chances of you meeting that person for which you're looking. So let's break down the phrase, "Exact behavior", and consider all the variables and ramifications that will up your "Odds" at attracting or finding that special person.

1. *KNOW* what you're looking for:

It's been mentioned, "If you don't know where you're going, how do you know when you get there?" Let's apply that truth to our situation here. Determine EXACTLY the kind of person that would make you happy, fit you like a glove, and match your level of energy along with personality. Remember, if they are JUST like you then there may be a conflict. So ask yourself the one big question, "If you could be another "You" in someone else's body of another sex, would you like to date them? Some of the most successful relationships are ones where the couples are vastly different in tastes, likes / dislikes, and views, but they both have the same CORE views about truth, sincerity, compassion, and credibility.

What is the definition of "Harmony?" Two forces, energy fields, or even musical notes that when combined bring about an effective end or pleasing result. Two musical notes that are just the right separation on the musical scale make a much more pleasing sound, than two notes or people singing the same note at the same time in a song. Some other examples are, where you're uninformed, they are more knowledgeable. Where they are weak, you're strong, and the examples are endless. The point is, in setting a goal as to the criteria of this "Just right" person, you should be carefully considering what would make you happy, write it down and SEE it as an already accomplished fact. JUST DO IT!

2. WHERE TO LOOK

WHERE you are looking is a very important factor in you finding WHAT you're looking for in the first place. If you were looking to buy a Ferrari sports car, would you go to the Chevy dealer? The metaphor here is exactly the same. If you are looking for someone who likes Western line dancing you don't go to a disco bar, and visa versa. You go to a place that features the amenities that attract that kind of person you want to meet. If you want to meet an "Upscale" type person who has achieved academic and vocational excellence, be prepared to spend $10 for a beer or your favorite beverage…and bring plenty of cash. As mentioned before, it usually boils down to one thing…"What do you bring to the table?" We will go into that later.

To sum it up, go to the type of place that YOU like to have fun in, that YOU like to enjoy and the chances of you meeting new people in general, that fit your personality and lifestyle will be greater than if you went to other types of places. Also remember when YOU'RE having a good time enjoying yourself, in a good mood, and have a very positive attitude, this attracts others of the same caliber, and attitude. Remember, **you attract what you are.**

3. HOW TO LOOK

How to look for that person that fits your parameters when you don't have a clue as to what they are about, what THEY are looking for, and what THEIR personality is, now that's ambiguous. The first thing that most people go by in choosing someone to approach, is that exact word…LOOKS.

LOOKS – HOW IMPORTANT IS IT?

This is something you may want to evaluate a long time BEFORE you begin "Looking". There is a very important concept to consider in your search. Which is more important, the ability to recognize the RIGHT person when they come along…or the ability to recognize the WRONG person before they attach themselves to you, become really difficult to break away from, and totally mess up your life? Once again, it's easier to know what you DON'T want sometimes than what you THINK you do want.

Looks or appearance, is the first thing that attracts two people the moment they first lay eyes on each other. The way their facial bones, skin, other structures are put together, and these "Looks" are the first attractants that cause two people to "Lock" on to each other. In that INSTANT evaluation each person makes about the other, as a result of these "Looks", several thoughts run through their minds.

THOUGHT #1: Is he/she good looking enough for ME to be seen with?

THOUGHT #2: Is he/she TOO good looking to be attracted to me, and am I good enough for them?

THOUGHT #3: What will my friends say when they see me with him/her?

THOUGHT # 4: Is he/she the right height for me?

THOUGHT #5: Will he/she like me or not?

All of these thoughts (more or less) run through a person's mind, at one time or the other, and when you complicate it with the multiplicities of BOTH people thinking the same things at the same time…it can get very complicated!

So what's the answer? RELAX…a relaxed attitude can put the other person at ease, and bring a state of relaxation to the entire interaction of both people. People tend to "Mirror" the person sitting in front of them, so if that person is "UP Tight", nervous, fidgety, that's what they are going to get back in a behavioral response.

Nothing says confidence like a relaxed attitude, and a smile that says, "Let's just have fun."

There are several "Layers" of looks or appearance, the outside is just one of them. When you realize the outside will change with time, but inside remains the same forever, you begin to look deeper into someone's inner personality, because that's what you'll be left with when the outside beauty is gone.

For 5 years I managed a singles club in southern California that was based upon athletics, if fact it was called, "Athletics Singles Association", and the main focus was putting single people together for sports, and social competition. It was amazing to see how much easier people got along and how relaxed they felt when they used the premise of "I'm just here to find someone to play golf, tennis, volleyball or whatever...with", and "I'm not really looking for a serious relationship". But...we were responsible for over 300 marriages in 20 years, so "Serious" relationships did develop. As you will usually find out, the harder you look for something the harder it is to find.

A major focus of this book is to teach you how to use your mental powers of visualization and materialization to DRAW that special to you or draw you TO that person you've been searching for. The second phase of the interaction is to REALIZE when they come along and how to react in a manner that will cause them to have more than a passing interest in you and create a mutual attraction for both of you.

It's a mysterious game where the ACT of trying, (to BE attractive) seems to *nullify or reduce* the level *of* attractiveness. In other words, many times TRYING to be cool or attractive is the very thing that turns people off. They can tell when you're just doing or saying something to "Make" you like them.

Take for instance most sports that are a one on one contest, where you are the only factor in winning or losing. It seems like the harder you TRY to win, the worse you play. It's when you just relax and LET yourself play, with the form and execution you've practiced, that you end up a winner with much less work and frustration.

So, the key here is to RELAX. People can sense when a person is "Trying" too hard to be liked, they talk too much, drink too much, are too animated in their actions, and it's obvious that they are going out of their way to impress you. NOT GOOD.

Once again, be yourself, because that's all you've got, and that is what will come out in the end no matter who you "Pretend" to be.

JUST DO IT!

CHAPTER 9

NON-VERBAL QUES & PROGRAMMING

The first thing we want to do here is define the term "Non-Verbal". Just by common sense deduction naturally you would think it's anything that is NOT verbal, and truly that is the best definition. So going further into the meaning, let's talk about the levels and "Types" of "Non-verbal-ness". Below the level of conscience awareness, is the meaning of SUB-conscience. Have you ever heard some say, "Subconsciously I probably WANTED to fail", or "My subconscious probably made me say it." When we make decisions, psychologists say that 80% of those decisions are made based on subconscious awareness. With that knowledge is it too much of a stretch to say that if you are aware of how the subconscious mind sends and picks up information that you can know much more about a person, from picking up these cues on a CONSCIOUS level. Your mind is always picking up cues about people around you, written and audio information, and then relaying this info to your conscious mind in the form of a statement about the subject of this info taken in. So let's talk about those NON-verbal cues as it relates to your interaction with other people, especially with someone with whom you would like to get to know, and possibly have a relationship in the future. It can be broken down in to several areas:

VISUAL CUES: These are things that you SEE, but because they are non-verbal you're not AWARE (on a conscious level) that you are actually seeing the information. Some of the reasons that you're not aware of seeing these cues are:

A) The visual stimulus is not DIRECTLY in front of you. Your subconscious mind picks up information very well on a 45 degree angle; in fact that is WHY it is conveyed subconsciously. Try this example test. When you're at a red light waiting for the green, do not look directly at the light. Look somewhere away from the light, but still keeping in your peripheral vision. The info that the light has changed will be relayed to your brain much quicker than if you were looking directly at the light. It's an old trick from racers at the drag strip when they are sitting on the race track waiting for the green light to GO! Many times the winner was determined by the car that got off the line the soonest after the light turned green.

EXAMPLE: A man and woman are sitting at adjacent tables on an angle from each other. Without actually looking directly at one and other each one can perceive that the other one is looking their direction or focusing their attention on the other one. Later a message is delivered to the conscious mind "She/He could be interested in me."

B) The visual info is right in front of you but you don't recognize is for what it is, because you are not picking up the cues or the cues are disguised. An example would be the old story of how the movie houses were flashing a picture of popcorn and soft drinks on the screen for just a blink of an eye in between the frames of the film they were showing. Suddenly people viewing this would become thirsty, and or hungry for popcorn. Later on this was declared illegal, but it illustrates how powerful subliminal programming can be, and how easily people could be influenced by subliminal methods.

Non-verbal **VISUAL** Cues

Once again because these cues are un-spoken they are called non-verbal and usually perceived by the SUB-conscious mind, then a message is sent up to the conscious as info to be considered.

1. Body Position - How a person stands or sits when interacting with you is a very strong non-verbal cue as to their level of attraction, agreement, or disagreement with you. We all probably know some of the signs, but let's take the obvious ones.

A) Defensive position: Arms folded in front of them. This is a universally recognized body position portraying a defense posture. It usually presents itself when someone hears something that they are opposed to, or disagrees with, in some manner, BUT...not always. It is also important that these cues discussed here are not cast in stone, and should NOT be taken as the ultimate bottom line truth in perceiving someone's stance or attitude toward you. They are just indicators of what COULD be, and most likely are.

BODY-POSITION

STANDING - NON-threatening

Hands at sides or clasped behind back, this is a good indication that this person is self-confident enough to not feel the need to be in a "Defense" mode, is relaxed in your presence and maybe even WANTS you to know this. So they stand or walk around with their hands behind their back.

BODY POSITION – SITTING

Legs crossed – If the direction of the upper calf is point TOWARD you or in your direction, it is generally a positive sign indicating that this person shows a positive interest in you. Once again this is not to be taken as gospel truth, maybe that person can't sit with their legs crossed toward you even if they wanted to, or maybe they had just spent a long time with their legs crossed away from you and now just switched positions to become comfortable while not indicating a positive attraction to you at all.

PREENING BEHAVIOR – WOMEN

Preening can be defined as any effort to make yourself look better, prettier, or more appealing. Some of these gestures may be adjustment of the hair, pulling the hair back from the front or sides of the face, application of new makeup, checking the appearance in a compact mirror etc.

EYE CHARISTICS - **IMPORTANT!**

Someone said "The eyes are the windows of the soul", and there is more than a gem of truth to that statement. The eyes of the person in front of you can tell you more than that person wants you to know about them, and it's impossible to disguise. You just have to be able to READ those signs, calculate the answers, and come up with a "Rebuttal" that will be the key to opening their "Personality lock". Here is a very important phenomenon you want to learn more about, and it's called, **NEURO-LINGUISTIC PROGRAMMING.** We will expound more on the advantages of NLP later in this book but for right now it's important to know a little bit about this part of "Body language" that will allow you to gain rapport with just about anyone man or woman. There are several different areas that eyes can "Tell their stories", and one of them is the amount of time that they eyes are focused in one place. YOUR TIME OF FOCUS is very important to sending a message.

One of the ploys of market research is the amount of time a customer's eyes stay locked on the product resting on the shelves. What the market researchers did, was to place a hidden camera within the shelving behind the products to record the length of time each person looked directly at the product in question. The longer they looked at the product, the more they bought the product. How does that translate to you gaining rapport with someone else. If you want to show someone you're interested in them, look into their eyes, and stay looking at them, DO NOT BLINK, and hold their gaze as long as possible. If THEY are attracted to you in the slightest, they will feel a greater rapport with you and have a positive feeling toward you instantly. They may even return your gaze in the same manner, which is to say, "OK, I'm interested in you too."

WHITES OF YOUR EYES

Do you remember the cartoons of the 50s when one of the characters would see something fantastic or the guy character would see the gorgeous girl and his eyes would almost explode out of his head. Actually there is some truth to that phenomena of the eyes bugging out when you see something that you really like or see something that really impresses you in a great way. It can be calculated by measuring the actual amount of white that is exposed in the eyes. When you are highly impressed with what you are looking at, your eyes will actually bug out just a little bit, and more of the white around your pupils will be visible. This is a visual characteristic that the "Trained observer" can pick up, or may be passed over by the casual observer. When it happens it is a obvious signal that whatever that person is looking at is something in which they are very interested. So, if you want to convey your interest or desire to cultivate a relationship with someone, practice "Bugging out" your eyes when you meet that person. It's usually done accompanied by the raising of the eyebrows, and flexing the eye muscles as you would if you were to intentionally cross your eyes forcing the eyeballs to protrude in the eye socket, showing more of the whites of the eyes. This is something you have to practice, (in front of a mirror) and REMEMBER to use when you want to gain rapport with that special person you are trying impress. It works like magic in attracting someone's approval or magnetically attracting them to you. It simply says, "I like what I see, and you're it."

EYE BLINK TECHNIQUE (Little known)

Here's a very little known "Trick" to gain rapport with someone. Watch their eyes, and determine how many times they blink per a 7 to 10 second interval. Then blink with them at the same time if you can. This is something that you REALLY need to practice with a friend before you try to use it in a "Real" situation, because it's almost impossible to carry on an "Intelligent" conversation while you are consciously thinking of blinking at the just right time. But, it CAN be done and it gives you immediate access to that person's mental computer, it's like getting their "Password" and now you're in and can program positive information about yourself and how much they are going to like you, what you do, and everything about you.

HAIR PLAY - WOMEN

This is constantly fiddling with their hair, twisting it around their fingers, tossing it from side to side, and in general just playing with it. Depending upon how often or how much attention they are giving this action can be an indication of lack of self-confidence and indecision, or just plain boredom.

AUDIO CUES

These are things that are actually said out loud, and some of them are conscious and some are Subconscious or intentionally imbedded in the conversation. The conscious cues are obvious complements like the things someone "Likes" about you, the clothes you wear, the way you wear your hair, other visual positive things about you.

If they are knowledgeable in embedding commands it may be not as noticeable. The subconscious mind perceives information in all manner of ways and directions. Researchers have proven that information given someone in reverse order, or backwards, upside down, is STILL received and computed by the subconscious mind.

EXAMPLE: In performing an experiment with embedding commands, I once said to a girl in a live music night spot,

*"I really enjoy **dancing**... (pause)**with me** it's swing music or old time rock n roll **that I like**...**you**...what kind of music to you like?"*.

I just embedded the command, "DANCE WITH ME", and "I like you" In just a few seconds she says, "Do you want to dance with me". That's an over simplification of the concept, but you can grasp the concept of embedded commands, and how effective they can be if you want to influence someone in being attracted to you.

All this is great, and it WILL give you an advantage in winning friends and influencing potential friends, but unless it is automatic, and delivered at just the right instant, it does you very little good. It's the automatic portion of behavior that is very difficult to master. That's why it takes considerable time and effort to practice to become very proficient so it doesn't SEEM like it is a learned piece of behavior, but just an automatic Reaction to the other person's behavior, and very spontaneous. You probably have met people just like this, but their behavior was not learned, not practiced, and just their natural reaction. That's called being SINCERE. That was just their natural state of behavior, that's why people liked them, and they got along well with everyone. Once you make these learned pieces of behavior part of your automatic responses, you will also have become SINCERE!

When all is said an done the ultimate goal is to cause someone that YOU have an attraction for, to be attracted to you, and to consider you a very desirous possibility as a potential friend, and later, have a possibility of a lasting relationship.

In the end, don't complicate things, simple is better, and a relaxed mannerism is relaxing to everyone around you projecting self-confidence. It says, "I'm enjoying my surroundings, I'm comfortable with myself and the people I meet, and I'm not TRYING to be cool, or impress anyone."

This is more for the men reading this, because once again they are the pursuers who initiate the beginning conversation. When a woman comes in contact with a guy like this, she recognizes him with a much higher degree in her evaluation of men. Why? Because men usually think they have to "Work" at being "Cool" and go out of their way to impress a woman, and when she encounters a man who doesn't do this, it puts him WAY up on the list of possible or potential men friends she may want to get to know.

Bottom line, just relax and let it happen.

CHAPTER 10

LUST AT FIRST SIGHT

AUTOMATIC ATTRACTION

This is sometimes called "Love a first sight" and although is happens VERY infrequently, it still does happen. You have two people in the same room or vicinity, who just happen to have a lot of the same values, beliefs, likes and dislikes. They meet and because of the same level of outward appearance (looks, height, hair color, facial structure) they are immediately drawn to each other. They begin talking and before long they find out in addition to being physically attracted to one and other, they are very much alike on many other levels. This should never be confused with:

LIKE ANIMALS

This is just animal attraction and many times it is only in one direction, meaning one person (usually the male) has a very strong attraction to the other person (usually the female).

EXAMPLE: A hot chick with a great body walks into the bar, restaurant, meeting place, and every guy in the places says, "I think I'm in love". Then the obvious question is, "With her, who wouldn't be"? This is the natural result when anyone sees something that they really, really, are attracted to, no matter what is in front of them. It's called EMOTION, and emotion trumps common sense 90% of the time. That's why people get involved with potential partners who don't work out, move in with those "Right now *potential*" partners, and break up with those "Shouldn't have been with", partners. Until you are the beneficiary of several experiences in the relationship category, and use these experiences to regulate or "Temper" your future actions, you most likely will be the victim of love…or lust…at first sight.

Along those lines, you know what they say about experience? *Good judgment comes from experience and a lot of that comes from bad judgment.*

People who have learned to think more with their head instead of their heart, (or other parts of their anatomy) have become much more successful at attracting, finding, and realizing the "Right one" when that person comes into their life. As they say, "You have to kiss a lot of frogs in order to find your prince." If you keep in mind that just maybe one of those frogs may NEVER turn *IN* to a prince, but may have the HEART of a prince, you have just graduated to the next level of decision making. This upper level of thinking will put you one step closer to making better choices, and ATTRACTING better experiences.

If you're really using your head, you'll notice some of the results of your close friends and family. Notice their successful choices along with the things and people that didn't work out the way they had it planned. "It seemed like a good idea at the time", is the usual response from someone who was thinking more with their emotional side, rather than their rational or NON-emotional side, when they describe relationship problems, or unsuccessful encounters.

Learning by experience is a tough way to learn new things and values. What you want to do is learn by OTHER PEOPLE'S experience or mistakes. It can be summed up the statement:

YOU WANT TO LEARN A LESSON WITHOUT HAVING TO PAY THE INSTRUCTOR.

In every lesson you learn you have to pay somebody, something, somehow for teaching you that lesson. In some cases the instructor is an inanimate object, like a tree, that you may run into while skiing, or worse…while driving too fast after too many drinks. A more positive example is that you MISSED the tree, didn't hit anything else, nobody was hurt. If you learned NOT to repeat that type of behavior (like drinking and driving) and nothing negative happened, then you learned a lesson and didn't have to pay "The instructor", consider yourself lucky. Remember, life is not a video tape, there is no rewind…no replay! Allow yourself to learn by someone else's mistakes. You will be way ahead in the game of finding that "Special person" you've been looking for without having to pay the price of wasted time, money, effort and frustration. Remember, it's all about CHOICES, and why you make them.

If you experience "Love at first sight", be careful, many times what you see is not

ALWAYS what you get, and all that "Glitters" is not usually gold. For each person you know, there is a price you have to pay to know them. It might take you some time to find out what that price actually is, then your choice will be, "Is it worth continued payment?"

That price may be extra effort and the amount of sacrifice it may take to reach and maintain a level of harmony between both of you. Many "Love at first sight" relationships burn out very quickly, because the "New" tends to wear off very quickly. Now you are left with the bare bones of what each person brings to the table, what they can contribute, and which "Little things" they do that you might not like, that may become big things after a while. It's been proven, the relationships that last a long time are the ones on a "Slow burn" of mutual attraction, give and take, and each person wanting the best for the other. They have an attraction for each other, but it's not this explosive, "On fire can't live without you baby" attitude.

The "Love at first sight" thing is a wild ride, but usually short lived, and much like a rollercoaster, with a lot of up's and downs. The trouble is, when you're just about to step up to get ON that ride, nobody, not even your best friends can persuade you to pass it by, even if they tell you the "Wheels" are not securely bolted on, and you're headed for trouble.

Take their advice and "***DON'T*** JUST DO IT!"

CHAPTER 11
CONFIDENCE

Nothing sells like confidence, and let's face it, everyone likes a person who is self-confident. They never try to hard to be liked, they always seem to say the right thing at the right time, and they don't talk too much when in a gathering or small group of people. Why is this, why are all the people with a good level of self-confidence easy to like, easy to get along with, and just seem to blend well with any and all types of personalities? Simple, because everyone likes some who "Seems" to know what's going on everywhere. They always have something interesting to say, they know the issues of the day, and they always seem like they are a step ahead of the "Herd".

Maybe we all can't have the level of self-confidence, but it's good to have that attitude of humble self-awareness, and just a little bit of the ability to know what is going on around you, and the ability to know when to "Shut up", and go with the flow, so to speak.

But, how do you GET this self-confidence,

when you don't know the surroundings, the "Lay of the land" and you are in unfamiliar territory?

One way to convey self-confidence if you are not sure of your methods, and procedures is to ASK QUESTIONS, let someone else guide you, give up control, and never try to pretend that you know something that you don't know. This impresses someone of the opposite sex, and tells them that you don't think you "Know everything". This also shows them that you are not so "Unbending" and set in your beliefs. This goes along way with making a favorable impression with anyone, especially a member of the opposite sex that you are feeling attracted to, and would like to possibly cultivate a relationship with in the near future.

The big question here seems to jump out at you, "How do you GET that confidence, when you've got nothing to build on, or have never done those things to give you a positive history on which to based your memories? Personal history is the builder, or destroyer of confidence. If you are a fighter and you've won every fight you've ever been in, you think you can't lose. That's why your manager has pitted you against opponents that are way below your ability. That manager wants to build his fighter's confidence, and the best way to do that is make sure he wins the first few fights as long as he performs reasonably well. Once this confidence is built up, he thinks he will do well against anyone he walks in the ring with, even if he is over matched. Belief is a very strong motivator, and as any winner will tell you, "Believe you can do it and you can". Someone said "It doesn't matter if you believe you can do something or your can't...one thing is true, YOUR'E RIGHT!

Being a winner at love, is no different than being a winner at anything you set out to do. There are certain parameters and variables that you need to get straight, and put into perspective. Then there is that little thing called luck, or fate when something happens that you didn't plan on and it provides a great opportunity on which you can, or should capitalize. Self-confidence draws these opportunities to you like a magnet, and it also helps you recognize these opportunities in time to take advantage of them.

If you were born "Good looking" then your personal history is probably a long string of getting any girl/guy you wanted, without a lot of work. If the opposite sex is beating a path to your door, then your level of self-confidence is naturally on a much higher level than the person who was not blessed with exceedingly good looks, wealthy parents, and a mind like Einstein, or Stephen Hawking.

At a very young age such as adolescence, "Kids" are more attuned to LOOKS rather than the quality of a person's personality, or level of credibility. So when your earliest memories of male/female interaction are being formed it's mostly based on physical attraction. Later in life when people "Grow up" (and some never do) our choices are tempered with characteristics beyond looks. By then we've learned (or should have) that great looks does not necessarily mean that someone is a great person, especially in all other areas that make up one's personality and or desirability.

But, back to the question of how do you GET

confidence when you're new to the "Game" of love, or dating, or just interacting with the opposite sex.

First of all let's examine the person whose personal history has not been all that great in their young life and might actually have somewhat of a negative personal history. This person has a considerable amount or "Work" to do to change this negative attitude.

Many times you've seen "Imbalanced" couples which generate comments like, "I wonder what she sees in him/her." Or, "She must be a really great cook", suggesting that there must be another reason that this couple is together other than "Looks". So what IS the reason for this situation, why do these people become attracted to each other? Could it be the fact that they have had a lot of personal history picking the WRONG type of person based on the WRONG type of criteria they may have been using, and the wrong set of values. Now they are using a different set of values other than LOOKS, material things or the "What can you do for me" scenario?

There are a lot of reasons why you come up with the mental synopsis that you, "Like" someone, and at first it IS looks, because that is what attracts you to someone to begin with, and makes your heart "Flutter' as they say. This is thinking with your animal instinct, your Libido, or the physical part of your being. Everybody does it, you can't help it, and it really is what attracts you to someone. It is very strange that certain people are attracted to certain body types and when in the presence of those body types they feel more attracted, and will throw all caution to the winds, give up all sense of rational behavior, and go GAGGA as they say. Who knows why this happens, is it in your DNA, is it written "in the stars?" In any case, somehow, some way two people are drawn together and they connect. The big realization is, DO THEY RECOGNIZE that they are meant for each other? The Universe has a way of trying to "Help" you in different areas of our life. If you don't recognize that help and take advantage of it, sometimes it passes you by, and it's a long time before you get another "Chance" like that again. The Universe, luck, fate, or whatever you want to call it, has a very strange characteristic when dolling out "Favors". If you USE the information, or you USE the HELP you have just received, then you tend to get more "Favors" or help. If you pass on the advance info, or do not USE the "Gift" bestowed on you, that kind of "Help" is subsequently diminished.

In other words, don't expect another "Gift" from the Universe if you don't use the one you're given.

The trouble with physical attraction is, that it's more than it's "Cracked up" to be. Sure, it's great to have a good looking mate, that makes all the other humans of the opposite sex go "Bonkers" over them, and say things like, "You lucky son of a gun", or "What has SHE got that I don't?"

If you focus 100% of your attention on appearance and physical attraction, then *you* better have a perfect body, great looks, and a great smile, because if that's what you're after, then that's what you should be "Bringing to the table of Attraction". Otherwise your "Table for 2" will be "Table for 1!"

CHAPTER 12

LEVELS OF ATTRACTION

Somebody said, "You can't go hunting bear with a slingshot", which illustrates the situation we are describing here. If you want to try to meet and get to know the most attractive girl/guy in the bar, you better be the most, or 2nd most attractive guy/girl in the bar, because people are attracted to someone on their own level/s. Which means their own level of intelligence, creativity, credibility, academic achievements, earning potential, and of course...LOOKS.

This is not to say that EVERY really good looking person will be repelled by someone who is below their level, or what they THINK is their level of looks, and achievement may be. Nothing is written in stone as far a personal attraction goes. Every day you will see a couple which looks miss-matched as far as "LOOKS" go. You may even make the statement, "Wow, she/he must be a REALLY great cook.", referring to a possible reason that someone of the opposite sex, which is way above the other partner (in looks and more) would be interested in that person.

So let's examine the possible reasons for the conception of the "Miss-matched" couple

1. HE BETTER LOOKING: He got her pregnant when they were young and her father had a large gun. Now they have several kids and need to stay together.

2. SHE BETTER LOOKING: He's got a lot of money and the ability to keep HER in a lifestyle in which she would like to be accustomed.

3. HE or SHE: Either one has had their fill of being with people just because of looks and realizes that what's inside can either make or break your happiness.

4. HE OR SHE: One of them does "Something" that the other REALLY, I mean, REALLY likes on a physical or mental level.

Back to the truth: *EMOTION TRUMPS COMMON SENSE EVERY TIME.*

I am sure there are many more scenarios, but

you get the idea supporting the statement, "Nothing happens without a reason."

Your success (or failure) in finding, or realizing that special person when they come along is largely dependent on looking beyond the physical appearance, and getting to know that person as best you can on as many levels as they will allow you to know. With that in mind as a guideline or parameter for choosing someone to cultivate a relationship with, you can make better more prudent choices when faced with the variables you come in contact with, in that search for the "Right one". Realizing that these are just guidelines, and nothing is cast in stone, you can start making your own set of values that fit your own lifestyle and goals. It also helps to realize that physical appearance and attraction is only temporary when viewed as our total time on this earth. Solid values, credibility, and compatibility are things that last a lifetime, and remain long after the physical attraction is gone. But then again that would be thinking with your logical side rather than your emotional side, so it just depends on how many times you have to be the "Bug" on the windshield of love, to start evaluating potential partners in a more realistic light. It's nice to be "On fire" with someone in a sparking relationship, but that spark means you can also get burned too. Usually the hotter the fire, the quicker it burns out.

So, somewhere in between, lies the answer you're searching for when it comes to choosing that person who you feel will be the "Right one". The key here is to REFINE your system of evaluation, and fine tune your "Filter" that separates right from wrong, the good from the bad and the "Really good" from the "Just OK." The question is, *how long* will it take you to come up with that finely tuned filter. For some people it takes years of experimentation, "Working on mysteries without any clues", and once you have all the "Filters" in place, will you LISTEN to them when they tell you, "This is not good", or they start ringing the alarm bell of "Run away NOW", from this person. Will you follow the path of "Emotion trumps common sense", and be the "Moth to the flame", or NOT?

Once again, it's all about choices, choose carefully letting your heart be guided by your common sense. You can always "Walk the plank" later if you really want to.

JUST DO IT!

CHAPTER 13

MOTH TO A FLAME

Yes, that's a famous euphemism that you hear all the time. It means simply that you like to toy with things that can kill you, or eat you up and spit you out like so much cannon fodder. You like to do this because of the unrealistic rewards you *MAY* encounter because of this interaction. Did you ever wonder how the casinos in Vegas can spend $500,000 on one sign. That is because they made $900,000 on people who thought they could *WIN* their rent money on one roll of the dice. The trouble is, they DID it ONCE...in 20 times, and they're stupid enough to think it can happen once again. There are always gamblers playing the "Long shot", drawing to an "Inside straight" (And if you know what that means, this chapter is for YOU) and it's these people who IF they were a moth, would definitely "Fly too close to the flame", and it would be...POOFF!

STORY:

upon a time, there was this man who met a girl he liked very much, he began and cultivated a relationship with her for a considerable length of time, but finally realized she wanted things he could not, or did not, want to give her. The trouble was, he really, I mean really, liked PART of her, but there was this other part/issue that was unacceptable. So they broke up...20 times. One minute she's praising him, telling him how much she loves him, and the next minute she's telling him what a bad man he is because he doesn't want to marry her, doesn't do what she wants him to do, and play this role she has planned for him in her life. He's like a moon around a planet, it has just enough rotational speed to keep it from being drawn in the gravitational field of the planet, but not enough speed to send it flying off into space, hence the definition of an orbiting planet.

Because he likes the "Good" part of their relationship SO much he can't admit that the objectionable part is something that will ALWAYS prevent the relationship from going forward toward the direction SHE wants.

This is the "Moth to a flame" scenario, and it happens over and over again in a lot of people's lives, because they refuse to realize that one, "Oops" wipes out 10 "Attaboyz". Sometimes it takes many negative occurrences, and many of those "Opuses" to make a person terminate the relationship knowing that the small little gem of what they like so much about the person of their affection, does not offset the negative aspect of the relationship. It's the simple law of "What do I get for what I give", and if the gap is too big, eventually there will be a break up. However, if the gap is close then it becomes like the "Sandpaper syndrome", Take a piece of sandpaper and rub it back and forth across your knuckle. Doesn't hurt too much...right away does it? Do it some more, and it becomes a little irritating. Keep doing it and when the top layer of skin comes away, you're in downright pain! (see chapter 20). In this instance, the small negative part no matter how small, begins to get "Bigger" when it keeps happening over and over again. One thing that you can do (if this describes you) is to establish an exact value of each of these areas in question. Let's say from 1 to 10 in terms of how closely that variable applies to you. 1 would mean it does not apply at all, and 10 would mean it's VERY important and ranks high in your life. Be very objective, the more honest you are, the more clear will be the picture you get from this evaluation. To save you time, here is the chart on the next page. As you may notice, some of the things in the positive column could also be considered negative by some people. Only you can give it a value. After you are finished add up the scores, and you may be surprised at what you've brought to light. Now come up with a score in your mind on how important *this* score actually is. Ask yourself the question, "Now what do I do with this information?

Here's a clue: **USE IT!**

POSITIVE	NEGATIVE
Exciting	Mundane
Honesty	Devious
Sexy	Non-Sexy
Adventurous	Boring
Sexual	Prudish
Non-Smoker	Smoker
Party Animal	Party Animal
Free Spirited	Too Laid Back
Children	Children
Geographical close	Geographical Close
Geographical Far	Geographical Far
Pets	Pets
Sports	Sports
Degreed	Non-Degreed
Job security	No Job Sec.

Remember, it's all about choices, and the more information you have at your disposal, the better choices you can make. The trouble with information that YOU supply is, it is sometimes very bias, and once again tainted with EMOTION. In repetition, we know the rule on emotion:

EMOTION TRUMPS COMMON SENSE EVERY TIME

Hopefully now you're learning a little bit about how to control that emotion, and have a higher "Vantage point" from which to view the "Lay of the land".

Let's say you are in a strange country or unfamiliar area, but can elevate yourself a mile in the sky, and you're looking at a set of train tracks. You can now see where the tracks go. Once you know where the tracks go, is there any reason you won't end up there when the train pulls into the station? So many people know enough about a person, and their personality, to be able to "Project" where the "Tracks" of their relationship with that person are headed, and it's not pretty. But like the

Moth to the flame, they get on that train knowing where the tracks go, and are somehow expecting to end up in a better or at least a different place at the "End of Track".

It's the woman who thinks, "He does things I don't like, but I can CHANGE him."

It's the guy who thinks, "I can't stand her smoking/attitude/temper/moodyness/etc.but what a body."

Don't be like the guy who finds out he took the wrong train going in the opposite direction, but he's having so much fun in the club car with new friends, he doesn't get off at the next stop!

If you *KNOW* where the tracks go, and you don't like were the tracks go, at least GET OFF at the next stop no matter how much fun you're having at the time!

Sooner or later you're going to come to "End of Track."

CHAPTER 14

FIRST DATES

We've talked about making a good first impression, remembering names, and using the information we've retrieved. Now it's time to put all that skill, and expertise to use. Some people say a first date is the most difficult time in the social interaction chain, and they could be right. This is where you make that first lasting impression, and you do it on many different levels, so let's break it down to those levels on which you have a chance to make an impression.

THE PHYSICAL LEVEL

This is basically how you look to the other person. It has to do with your grooming, clothes, physical characteristics, and how you carry yourself. The more time (up to a point) you spend preparing yourself, the better chance you have of presenting your "Best side", if you want to call it that. We all have this opinion of how we look to other people, mainly because we have something in our house called a mirror. By the way some people look, or present themselves, you may think they DON'T have a mirror...anywhere, but that's another chapter. Speaking of mirrors, if you can get a double mirror situation in your bathroom/make-up room, it would be of some great help.

DOUBLE MIRROR: There is a main mirror on the wall in front of the sink, and another as a door of a medicine cabinet just to the right or left on the nearest wall. If you open the mirrored door to the medicine chest at just the right angle you get a profile view of yourself, and how you look when people see you at a 90 degree angle, which can be a real eye opener. It gives you a profile view of how that new haircut, or hair-doo looks from the side. You'd be surprised sometime when you give yourself a quick check and realize there is a wild "Cow lick" sticking up in back, or something else that would send the opposite sex running for cover, from YOU!

MEN: Shaving

Depending on your age, to shave or not to shave. In the more modern "Up to date" age it's

"Cool" to have a 3 day beard. For mature men courting more mature women it may be better to be close shaven. I always figured if I looked like a homeless guy, this is not going get me any points, and if I am clean shaven, I at least look like a productive member of society with a job.

Women tend to like men that actually have a job, earn money, make a house payment, drive a car that starts without being pushed, and spend a little of that $$ on THEM. To them it all adds up in the end with a "Security rating", on how well you can provide for them...and usually their child or children (depending upon their age).

At any rate, you probably have a good idea of the image you want to project, to attract the kind of woman you're looking for, but proceed with the goal of keeping it simple, clean, and productive.

MEN: CLOTHES

The way you dress says more about you than almost anything else you could do. The first thing you've got to do is take stock of what kind of body you're living in. Obviously if you haven't got a gymnast's physique, and you've got a few extra pounds in the wrong place (as if there's a right place) you don't choose a tight fitting tapered, "V cut" athletic, WHITE, shirt and pants. Once again you really have to wonder if some people actually do have a mirror anywhere in their house. But back to clothes, someone once said, "Clothes make the man", I don't totally agree, although I do believe that clothes make you NOTICE the man. HOW you notice someone can only be classified in a positive manner or a negative manner. It's this impression that you are left with, that is very hard to change once it's been stamped into someone's brain. Someone also said, "You can't put lipstick on a pig", oh you could but you'd still have...a pig. What I'm trying to say is the right clothes can help your image, but there IS a limit on what it can do. There is a prominent talk show host who is supporting quite a few extra pounds, and he looks terrific in his $2500 custom handmade suits, because they are a perfect fit...and all dark colors.

MEN:COLORS

WHITE: Some colors hide things and some accentuate things. For instance, the color white will bring out every overweight ounce of belly fat, and "Anywhere fat" you may be trying to hide, so unless you're going to cover it with a vest, suit coat or sweater, stay with the neutral or darker colors.

BLACK: This is your friend if you've got a few, or a lot, of extra lbs. It masks the bulges and overall girth you may be balancing above your knees, and works well to minimize your overall size. It also lends a distinguished air of serious credibility. If you want someone to take you serious, don't dress in multi-colors like a clown.

BLUE: A blue shirt is a sign of credibility, and truth. "True blue" is what generally pops into someone's mind when you're wearing a blue shirt, possibly tan pants, it's a good combo. Did you ever notice what color that presenter of just about ANY product you see in a TV commercial is wearing...BLUE! It is not just happen stance, or because they didn't have anything else to wear that day, it works to sell their product, and it will work to help you sell yourself to the opposite sex or anyone else for that matter.

RED: Whoa now, this is a strong color, NEVER wear red if you're going to try to project an image of harmony and relaxation, it screams "I'm a controller". This is a sign of power, and control, and would work good in negations, but not a point getter on the first date. In this case it may be a little over the top and says, "I'm trying to make a statement here". Maybe the best statement to make on a first date is, "I'm not trying to impress anyone...yet." The fastest way to lose credibility with someone is to come off as someone "Trying" to make an impression. Then you're labeled as someone "Trying too hard", to be liked, to be...whatever.

GREY: Now here is a color that says "Credibility, I don't need to impress you, and I'm keeping a low key attitude." It is what you'd want to wear to a corporate sales meeting, or taking a client to lunch. Not a great first date choice, but you could still pull it off if you're James Bond.

The colors you choose should reflect your mood, and the mood you think people will be sporting around you for the day or evening. Parties, dinning out, bar hopping, the beach, all these are fun casual events that you need to dress in harmony with, and match that level of energy. When you are thinking about what to wear for an occasion or event, it basically falls into a few main areas: casual, or formal, work or play, it's hard to pick something out of order, (if there was any order to those things) unless you choose with your eyes closed, and be too "Out there on the fringe". For these venues, just pick something you LIKE, that hopefully won't make people think you're TRYING to get noticed.

CHAPTER 15

LISTENING

I'm sure you've been in situations with people who make you just want to stand up and shout, "Will you please shut up for 5 seconds!" This person is obviously not what you would classify as a "Good listener". It's been said that, "God gave you 2 ears and one mouth"...for a reason. That reason was to imply that you should LISTEN more than you talk. Some people however have never learned that rule, and once again it comes under the umbrella of "Trying too hard" when someone dominates the conversation, wants to tell, tell, tell, and thinks that everyone somehow CARES, about them and about the subject on which they're expounding.

If you want someone to be attracted to you, and keep from being bored while with you, *TALK LESS THAN THEY DO!*

Some people listen alright, but they're just listening for the spot where the other person stops for a second to take a breath so they can start talking again. NOT GOOD!

Here are some rules for social interaction that will make you more attractive to anyone, let alone that member of the opposite sex with whom you're trying to get to know.

1. ASK QUESTIONS: There is no better way to get to know someone than to ASK them about themselves. This will result in you talking less, and getting info about their likes and dislikes, but most of all stimulate more conversation from them than you. People love to talk about themselves and it makes them feel good to bring up their accomplishments, accolades, and triumphs. It also shows a genuine interest coming from your side of the conversation, which is a plus for you in their eyes.

2. START/STOP PAUSE: This is something that will make people attracted to you like a magnet! Many times someone will pause or stop their words in an effort to search for the right phrase or word to describe something. If you wait and allow just a second gap between the time they quit talking and you START talking, this gives them time to finish their thought if they are not yet done with their comment or sentence. There's nothing worse that trying to explain a concept or situation and be interrupted before you're finished. This does not make points for you in a first impression.

3. LISTEN TO THEIR WORDS: Specifically this means listen to the descriptive words they use and the way in which those words fit into a sentence. I have, and will talk considerably about NLP (Neuro-Linguistic Programming) and how it opens new window of communication and understanding between people. The WORDS people use can give you a "Road map" of how to be successful in communication with any kind of person/personality.

VISUAL: If they use a lot of words like LOOK, SEE, SEEING, APPEARS, SIGHT, VIEW, and words that relate to the way you SEE things, you are probably dealing with a VISUAL biased person. If you want them to relate to you, use those visually related words and phrases back to them in conversation.

Ex: "I SEE what you're talking about", or I SEE your point, "You APPEAR to be correct", I like the LOOK of this".

AUDIO: This person uses words like HEAR, SOUNDS GOOD, RINGS BY BELL, I HEAR YOU, MUSIC TO MY EARS, I'M ALL EARS, this person will not relate well to someone who says things like, "Can you *see* what I'm saying", but will relate to phrases like "You're going to love the *sound* of this", or "That rings true". They also are a more lower keyed type of individual, they talk slower, softer and are good listeners. Once again, talk less, listen more, ESPECAILLY with this person.

FEELING: This is classified as "Kinesthetic" in the NLP world, and it means simply that this person organizes their life mainly around the way they FEEL, more than sight, or sound. They use phrases like, "This has a good FEELING", or "I've got a good HANDLE on it", or "I'd like to TOUCH on that for a moment". This also is a person who is VERY soft spoken, and subdued in their actions, speech, and places a lot of "Gaps" in their speech patterns. You had better look for these gaps and don't "Step" on them, because that will turn this person against you very quickly. Lower your voice, slow down with this person, and give them time to respond to your question or comments. If you do you'll make an instant friend, if you don't, they'll be looking at their watch very frequently.

TOTAL SILENCE: If you don't have something to say, don't say anything. This applies to the time when you are in a confined space, like driving on a trip, watching TV, relaxing or whatever. Sometimes it's nice to just have things quiet, and if you can realize that moment, or situation when it comes along, and react with NO TALK, this will go a long way with a lot of people. It follows the school of thought, "Less is more". Some situations like this are if someone is reading, studying, absorbed in an action requiring their concentration, or they just want it quiet for a while. Learn to recognize this and react properly, and you will become more attractive to someone this way, than if you try to fill the void with "Useless verbiage".

PROOF OF LISTENING

Some people do a thing called "Play listening", which means they contribute just enough response to "Sound" like they are actually listening. This means putting in a "Ah Ha", or "Um right" or "Yep", in at what they would consider the appropriate points of the conversation, even though they haven't heard a word that's been said. This may work up to a point, until the other person asks them a question about what is being discussed, and all they can say is, "Do what now"?

If you HAVE been listening in a proper manner you can interject a few responses to let the other person know you are with them in the conversations, and this we will call, "Proof of listening", and it goes a long way with achieving rapport with someone.

If you've done a proper job of listening, then it will be no problem to contribute meaningful information to the conversation. This means that when you do speak up that you've got something to say that adds value to your time together, and helps you get to know someone.

TALKERS

Some people are what we will call "Talkers", which means they just can't bring themselves to throttle down in a conversation or group gathering. In this case it is not because they are trying to impress someone, or boast about their accomplishments, they just talk too much. They've always been like this, and they will probably always be like that for the rest of their life. They've probably been in sales, or some kind of job where it was necessary to be explaining technical data, or instructions etc. This then transfers over to their non-sales part of life, and becomes a way of interaction for anyone that they come in contact with, or any conversations into which they enter.

If this describes you, and you want to win friends, influence people, and in this case attract that special mate, LEARN how to listen. It may be one of the most difficult skills you can acquire, but it will pay big dividends later on, and not just with members of the opposite sex, but all social as well work situations.

If you're a "Talker" and want to seriously make a change in your behavior, then set down some goals to work toward. Below are some examples.

GOAL 1: Let the other person talk for at least 60 seconds without you saying anything.

GOAL 2: Listen to what they are saying intently, and formulate an intelligent question you can ask about their last or one of their last remarks.

GOAL 3: Have face to face contact with them at least 3 times during the conversation (if possible).

GOAL 4: Try to learn enough about them to

find a common ground between you both.

GOAL 5: **Remember their name!** This tells the other person that you value their presence enough to remember who they are. There is nothing more embarrassing than to part company with someone after only a short time and have to ask their name a 2nd time.

Keep these goals in mind every time you engage someone in a conversation, no matter what sex they might be, do this as practice, just to teach yourself the skill, and you will begin to make that change that will transform your ability to attract that special person.

Remember to *remember*...to JUST DO IT!

CHAPTER 16

FIRST IMPRESSIONS

Well, we already talked about "Never getting a second chance to make a first impression", so now let's go in to more detail of how to structure conversation, project an image (without looking like you're trying to do that), and bottom line, make an indelible branded impression on someone's inner mind that will filter information up to their conscious awareness, saying "I like this person".

So how do you go about making this lasting impression, when you've got only one shot at getting it right? First of all, RELAX...take the pressure off yourself, and take the attitude of, "If He/She doesn't like me it's their loss, I'm a likeable person, got my own thing going on and if they can't see it, they don't deserve me".

In a world of "Players" that try to fabricate their accomplishments, possessions, and puff up their image to the breaking point, you will rise above the masses that think that "This is the way it's done"...NOT!

People in today's single marketplace have become more aware, and more sophisticated in their search-and-find efforts. They've got the...***INERNET!***

However; you need a lie detector to wade through all the "Semi-True" info that is floating around out there. They say that pictures don't lie, WRONG, they may be pictures of that person 10 years ago, or, a picture of someone else!

So what's the secret of making a great first impression? BE YOURSELF! The minute you try to be someone else that you're not, there's missing information in your "Resume" that you've got to fill in on the spot, in a second's notice, and you're saying things like..."Well I ah, don't actually *WORK* there with so and so, and I ah, I did such and such for only such and such for a short time ...YOU'RE BUSTED! First impression...GONE!

People can't stand a "Phony", and if you're not happy with the "Real" person you are, CHANGE IT! Then you won't have to remember things that were never there in the first place.

Everyone wants to appear better than they are...why? Because they're always *looking for someone* that is "Better than they are", instead of someone that can contribute something I've always harped on, called "Natural harmony".

Natural harmony is when two people don't have to "Try" a lot to make their relationship work. They give each other the space they need to be themselves, but provide the support to keep the other person in the "Pocket", in their "Groove", and help upright them if they get a little "off center". They always want the best for the other person, whatever that means. If that means one person goes "Out with the Boys/Girls", or their friends, separately...then they realize you should have that time to be with your friends, to share good times with just those people. If means time by themself, then do that. To make a good 1st impression, if you exhibit an attitude of Non-Control and flexibility in a potential relationship, it is going to go a long way to making a great first impression.

When you have that attitude, you WILL make a great 1st impression. One that will be implanted into someone's mind as "I like this person, they're for real!"

So make a great first impression by letting the other person talk more than you do, ask questions about them, and RELAX! You can't MAKE someone like you, the harder you TRY, the more they will see you ARE "Trying", and run the other way, perceiving you as a "Needy" person. There goes your 1st impression.

If they like what they see, if they like what they hear, if they like what they feel...they'll be back. The trick is (if there is a trick) drawing them to *you* rather than you going to them.

CHAPTER 17

SEXUAL ATTRACTION

or LOVE VS. LUST

So just what is it that attracts two people when they come in close proximity to each other?

We talked about this Love vs. Lust earlier, but let's go into the nuts and bolts of how it happens on a physical level. What are the things that attract two people?

SEXUAL RELEASERS :

These are things that trigger attraction or repulsion in the human sexual or interactional experience. When members of the opposite sex come in contact with each other they are either attracted, are neutral, or are repelled by a number of physical bodily factors exhibited by each person. Some of them are:

1. HEIGHT: There are two aspects of height to consider here, and the first one is, how tall is HE in relation to HER. For each person this is a different releaser. Some women just like tall men, they are most likely tall themselves, but not always. A man's height, for women, has for thousands of years meant security, protection, and safety. It projects strength, leadership, and all that goes with it. Very few men, unless they are tall, are attracted to women who are taller than themselves. The man is suppose to be the dominant figure in the cave, tent, the Tepee, the home or the mansion. How can he do this if his woman is taller the he?

Some men are secure enough in themselves to never let this be a factor, some make it a major problem. Each person is different. The same goes for women in being attracted to the male. Some feel it's important, some don't.

2. BODY TYPES: What "Types" of bodies are there?

Athletic: This is the physically in shape, just right weight for the height of a person. Nothing is too big or too small where it shouldn't be. Everything is just the right size for the person's height and weight. In women the "Parts" are not overly large but not exceedingly small, the legs are not "Skinny" but also are not too muscled, or large. In trying to describe this body type the difficult term used here is the word..."TOO".

What may be considered "TOO" big or small for one person, may be just right for another. What comes to mind in this case is the phrase, "Beauty is in the eye of the beholder." With this in mind most people still have a judgmental level of what is OK, REALLY NICE, and SPECTACULAR!

Gym User: WORKOUT WILLIE or WILMA This is one step above the athletic body, slightly enlarged arms, legs, neck, all above average size. In women it's a masculine look, and it's obviously something they feel they need to do. It just depends upon the type of person you want to attract, how you develop *your* body and the time you want to spend in that developmental stage.

Weight Lifter: Mr./Ms. America Type - This person has spent a lot of time at the gym, drinking protein shakes, and performing muscle building additives. Pick any spot on their body and it's TOO big, compared to the athletic type. But, still there are some people (men as well as women) that find this greatly attractive. It all depends on where your priorities are, and what you want to DO with your body in relationship to *why* you want to change it. Do you want to develop your bicep so you can hit yourself in the face harder? Because that's the motion you use with a heavy weight in your hand in developing your biceps. You've got to ask yourself, why do you want to develop your body to be twice as big, and twice as strong as a normal athletic person? If it's because it's your life long dream to get a job as a bouncer in a nightclub, or win a UFC Championship, then by all means...go ahead on!

Slightly out of shape: This body type belongs to the over 40 crowd, the guy who USE to be the star athlete in high school, the 4 minute mile runner, or the cheer leader who had a perfect body, ONCE. Later they got bogged down with the job, the house, the kids, but still makes it to the gym, or the tennis court, 2 or 3 times a week and walks the 18 holes in golf. Gets his/her heart rate up 2 or 3 times a week, and says, *"I'm not as good as I once was, but I'm as good once as I ever was."* Which is the title of a country song by Toby Keith, look it up, you'll love the video.

No hope Harry/Harriet: They've given up a long time ago when they thought the scale just needed repairing. Most of their weight is below their belt, or middle, and on their legs. You probably won't find this body type in the disco or nightclub, but you will find them at the pastry section in the grocery store. As far as "Sexual releasers", well that ship has sailed!

FACEUAL CHARICTARISTICS

EYES: The eyes are a very powerful sexual releaser in attracting a member of the opposite sex. In women the size of the eyes are a sexual arousal trigger to the male. You've heard the term "Deer eyed girl?" In case you don't know, deer have quite large eyes. Now with the new cosmetics in eye makeup almost any woman can have those "Come hither" eyes, that flash the "I'm available" signal to the male whose already going gaga over her smile, providing she has all of her front teeth.

In the male the eye color can be a sexual magnet. There's nothing like a pair of piercing blue eyes to get her to say "Yes" to a dance with you, and several other things later on.

In women a pair of "Baby blues" can be devastating to the unsuspecting male, like a spider to a fly, drawing him in to her spell of visual intoxication.

Another combination of eyes that can be hypnotic is the green eyed Irish girl with red hair. Since you focus mostly on the eyes when you are conversing with someone, this is a tremendous sexual releaser for both sexes. The amount of times you blink when you are really interested in someone becomes less and less the more you are attracted to them. They are subconsciously noticing this and a message is sent up to their conscious mind, "I think this person likes me".

The amount of time you hold someone's eyes (without blinking) when you first meet them, sends them a message saying, "I like you...I'm attracted to you...I want to get to know you." If they do the same, it says the same thing to you.

TEETH: This is a no brainer, if you see someone with perfect teeth, it tells you they had parents that valued dental improvement, had the money to spend on braces when they were young. Nice teeth give someone a nice smile, and a smile says so much about a person before you even get to say hello. On the other hand poor teeth and bad dental hygiene are ultimate turn-offs for most people so if this is your problem, get it fixed or get nixed.

COMPLEXION

Different people like different things, and this holds true for complexion. Some people like a complexion with a great tan, others like a fair complexion. It's interesting to know how the attractant of this variable has changed through the years. In the middle ages the phrase, "She is the fairest in all the land", meant someone came from a high level of aristocracy. Someone with a extremely fair complexion was never out in the sun, which in turn meant they never did manual labor, or left the castle.

Now when we see a pasty white complexion most people think, "Hey girl/guy, why don't you get some sun on that body. Just the reverse of what was perceived in the middle ages is now viewed as a affluent life style. If you have this white pasty complexion it means you probably work all day in an office, and only come out after the sun goes down. If you have this lovely golden tan it means you're probably retired, playing tennis, relaxing at the beach or pool side all day long, and projects a high level of health and vitality, along with a possible affluent lifestyle

UPPER BODY - MEN

If you are a man, the shoulders, chest, neck, and arms are sexual releasers. Broad shoulders instantly convey an aire of masculinity, and strength to a woman. Just the opposite is true, skinny undeveloped arms, long skinny neck, narrow shoulders project, computer nerd, pencil neck geek (Dr. Demento) to the opposite sex, and lower opinion of same.

LOWER BODY - MEN

Stomach: If you have a "Six pack" type stomach or abs, you're going to score high in any woman's book, but this is quite non-typical in men, unless they spend a lot of time at the gym. Since most men don't walk around without a shirt, the lack of six pack abs hasn't really become a biggie, as long as there is no accompanying "Spare tire".

However, the presence of a large beer gut is the ultimate turn off for most women, unless of course they have a matching belly without being pregnant. Then you may have a match, "Made in heaven." Remember, you attract what you're like. This is one rule of the Universe you should never forget. If you don't like the type of person you attract, take a better look at yourself. Why do you think all the walls of a health & fitness club are lined with MIRRORS?

UPPER BODY - WOMEN

BREASTS: Well, do we have to go into this area or is there anything that anyone has to be told about this area of a woman's body in relation to being a sexual releaser for men. Large breasts are obviously a turn-on for men, and there are probably NO men that would say this area is not a turn-on. They (breasts) however, cannot be accompanied by a large stomach, which for most men (unless they have the same problem) is a major turn-off. For some men breasts are important, for some they're not. Either you're a breast man, or a "Leg man", if you want both, then you need to move to Hollywood, have a perfect body, and get into "Adult movies."

LOWER BODY - WOMEN

LEGS: This is a very subjective area as sexual releasers for men. Some men like well developed legs, like ice skaters, or tennis players. On the other hand, some men prefer women with more slim legs or "Runners" legs. It all depends what you find attractive, only you know what this is, and what "Rings your bell."However, once again, you attract what you are so if you have a good body, then you can attract a good body, and you probably will be attracted TO someone of the opposite sex who has the same type of body. Height, athletic, etc. The trouble is, with most people that DON'T have an "In shape" body, they STILL want someone who IS in shape and that's where the problems start.

Stand in front of a mirror naked, and say to yourself..."This is they TYPE of person I will attract." If you want someone/something better you've got to change *into* something better. JUST DO IT!

CHAPTER 18

GETTING LUCKY

Since *part* of the title of this book is, "It's NOT just getting lucky", let us try and define just what luck is, how to attract it, what to do with it when you DO get it, and how to know when it DOES come to you. First of all, you have to examine the concept of LUCK. What is luck in the first place?

One dictionary definition of luck: *Success or failure brought about by chance, rather than one's positive, or negative, actions.*

Luck: It's when something unexpected happens that was unforeseen, good or bad, in this case good, you had absolutely no control over it, and you are the beneficiary of it. We will call that good luck. So what are we talking about when we say, "Getting lucky in love"? That term to some men, has come to mean, meeting a girl, and having an intimate or sexual experience with her shortly after they meet. Sometimes this turns into a long-term relationship, sometimes not. In this case we're using the term to denote finding someone, in that monstrous sea of people and personalities that fits you and your personality very well.

If you look at the Yin & Yan symbol you will notice where half of the symbol is thin, the other half right next to it is thick and visa versa. In this instance we are talking about finding someone who fills your "Empty" space, is up when you're down, picks up your slack, and wants the best for you all the time, and in return you do the same for them. As mentioned before, that would be called "Natural harmony", when you don't have to bend over backwards to make a relationship work. THEN you can say you "Got Lucky".

You've heard the term, "Lucky stiff", denoting a person who always seems to have good things happening to them. They seem to be born under a "Lucky star", and they never seem to have to work at life in general. In high school they never seem to study to get top grades, they are a winner at sports, went with the best looking cheerleader or football star, everybody wanted to be their friend, and the world was their oyster. With all that in mind let's dissect this person's life and maybe see what brought all this about. Just for the sake of illustration, let's call these people "Roberta and Robert.

1. First lucky event: A very good looking man a woman decided to marry and have children, Roberta and Robert. This event we have to classify as LUCK! Who knows what mysterious force in the Universe caused these two people to be drawn together at the same place, same time, and decide that they liked each other, but that's what you call luck. It was probably the same force that caused THEIR two parents to meet, and produce them. Roberta and Robert turned out much like their parents, good looking, intelligent, AND with common sense too.

2. Second lucky event: Their parents had money: Because they were intelligent, became professionals in their fields, made good investment choices, and they had the funds to finance the kids' higher education. From that point the kids went to excel in professional fields of their own, and went on to re-create the American dream that they were raised in, and to what they had become accustomed.

Once again we have seen the face of LUCK

present itself in two people's lives. However, when you think about the entire scenario you must realize that much of that luck was generated by the CHOICES made by the people involved in the story. This book is more about CHOICES, and how to make the right ones, along with how to increase your chances of attracting GOOD luck, as well as the perfect person for you and you alone.

Within the same vein as luck, let's explore the other side of the equation of "Not so good" luck. A child is born of average parents, average in looks, intelligence, financial standing, and a TREMENDOUS amount of common, or "Street" sense. Let's call him "Sonny". Sonny's parents split up when he was young and he stayed with is Grandmother, the only bit of luck he had, was that he possessed a higher degree of intuitive perception. He was good at sifting through the chaff, and coming up with the best solution quicker that anyone else. Because of this trait in making the right choice in many different situations, Sonny attracted, and actually manufactured his own, "Luck". Once again, it's all about choices, and the choices you make sometimes follow you the rest of your life. Like that tattoo you got after you drank too much, that said, "Booze is the only answer". It was a *permanent reminder of a temporary feeling*, which is the title of a Jimmy Buffet song. Look it up, you'll love it!

You've heard someone say, "He/she is a accident waiting to happen", or "They are a magnet for disaster." This is a person who constantly pushes the "Envelope of reality." They expect their friends (if they have any) to pick up their slack, as well as the check at dinner. Very simply, they ATTRACT bad luck because of their CHOICES. If you want to "Get lucky", and attract the most perfect person for you, then first of all you need to RECOGNIZE them when, and if they come along. This once again comes under the umbrella of choices.

It all depends on your criterion for what is "Right", and why you have arrived at this set of standards. When you are setting these standards, or goals for what that perfect person should be like, ask yourself, "Are they in the envelope of possibility for what I have to offer?"

If you're over weight, need dental work, live with your parents, and are wondering if your bus pass is expired, is there any possibility of you attracting a young attorney, driving a Bentley, who looks like a movie star? At some time you have to face facts, take stock of your assets, liabilities, and if you don't like what you see...*DO SOMETHING ABOUT IT!*

MAKING YOUR OWN LUCK

Now here is where you either keep going the direction you're going, or change that direction in a manner to bring you to a new state of being, assuming you don't like the state of being you're in now. It's been said, *"If you don't know where you're going, how do you know when you get there"*. Let's examine the statement, "Making your own luck", and look at another statement, which says, "Chance favors a prepared mind." Being prepared sometimes means just being AWARE of your surroundings and choices.

PREPERATION CAUSES EXPECTATION

This is simply preparing for something that you EXPECT to happen. You expect it to happen because you've pictured it happening, and you have faith it will happen so much that you MAKE it happen.

Once upon a time, there was this band that played all kinds of music, and they had come to a place of boredom with their music. They weren't getting any playing jobs, they needed money and were lamenting on what to do. The band leader, a very insightful dude proclaimed, "Ok guys, we're going to learn some new songs, and start to re-light the spark of energy and focus on being the best band we can be."

There was a great amount of groaning, complaining, and saying things like, "We don't have any jobs on which to play new songs, so why should we do all that work and put forth all that effort?"

The band leader being a skilled taskmaster told them forthright, that they would get no more beer, drugs, or sex, (because they had no more money to buy those things) until they learned these new songs, of which he had a detailed list.

In a few weeks after learning these new songs, while creating a stronger bond between each other, they were invited to play in a "Battle of the bands" at a local state fair. One of the first required songs they were to play was one of the new songs they just had learned, and they blew people away with their rendition of it. Every one was so impressed that they voted the band, "Best of show" and now they had their pick of jobs. A talent agent was in the crowd who picked them up as one of his acts, and they ended up opening for a major world famous band, and was asked to go on tour with them. They performed one of their original songs, and was asked to record it, and it eventually hit number one on the charts. They now have their own record label, and can buy all the beer, drugs, and sex they could ever want, but that's another story called "Managing your assets/Over indulgence. Why did this all happen? They put the effort in before they knew they NEEDED to, and were ready for what they wanted to have happen BEFORE it happened. Which is the definition of being...PREPARED!

EXPECT the results you are wanting to have happen so much that you prepare for it BEFORE you think you really need to. HAVE FAITH: If you expect the results you are wanting, then do something to demonstrate that expectation. This is called EXPECTATION FAITH in you being prepared. This is the thing that gives your expectations power, and makes things happen.

Remember, "You get what you think about most", per the book, "*Laws of Attraction.*"

In my little home town in Illinois I remember people showing up at church to pray for rain because of draught, and even though there wasn't a cloud in the sky, everyone was carrying a UNBRELLA. That's called faith.

If you want to attract that special person for whom you've set some standards as criterion goals, then start making your own luck by being prepared. Lose that extra 15 or xx pounds you've been toting, make an appointment with your barber or hair stylist, buy a new piece of clothing that gives your persona a lift. Feeling good also means feeling positive, and feeling positive attracts other positive things, people, and events.

GET PREPARED!

APPEARANCE AXIOM: Per Dion Sanders the football player: *"If you look good, you feel good. When you feel good, you play good. When you play good, they pay you good."*

I'll submit, when you look good, you feel good, and when you feel good, you attract good things, good events and positive people. That's the way positive energy works to attract good luck, and the same is true in reverse. It's called the "Spiral of luck". A spiral either goes up or down, but never stays in the same place, which means good luck just gets better and bad luck gets worse. *NEVER* go out in public looking less than your best! You'll be ready for the time when that "Right" person comes along, and they WILL come along. The Universe has a funny way of rewarding a prepared mind, or "Teasing" an unprepared mind or poor preparation, and it WILL happen to you! ALWAYS BE READY!

CHAPTER 19

ARE YOU READY?

So now you've dropped that extra weight, got a great "Doo", and a new shirt/top/pair of shoes or whatever, and you're ready for anything the Universe throws at you. Trouble is...you don't see any incoming "Pitches", or incoming, anything. You're thinking, "Where's that materialization of what I'm waiting for?" As you go through life you'll begin to realize that the Universe is very unpredictable in specifics. So what would you label here as "Specifics?" Here's one way to look at it. The Universe is "Self-leveling", which is to say it is like water. If you put two containers of water together connected by a tube at the bottom, and pour water in one of them, the water will flow into the other container until BOTH containers have the same level of water in them.

To put that premise into an explanation of how the Universe works in a general sense, if you TAKE from someone else, or the Universe, either by permission (meaning a gift) or by theft, and don't make repayment, the Universe will TAKE from you in some way, usually commensurate with what you received FROM that person or the Universe. I say "Usually" because that's where the system goes slightly off track, or the unpredictability of the Universe comes in to the equation. Sometimes it may pay you back 10 times what you had taken from you, or what you put INTO the Universal Bank by helping someone and not getting paid directly for it. On the other side, may take 10 times what is *owed* from the cheater with whom you were involved. The Universe has the predictability of a cat, but the GENERAL rules always apply. You get back what you put in, sometimes more.

The reason for this side track of explanation is to illustrate the fact that just because you do all these positive things to increase your "Luck quotient" with attracting the opposite sex, don't throw it all under the bus because it hasn't happened right away. You've created the "Ready environment" now just keep picturing the end result all the while KNOWING it's going to happen.

Let's further illustrate this with a little scenario

like a baseball game. You stand there at the plate waiting for the pitch, but no pitch comes. You wait and wait and wait, and...nothing. So you take a more relaxed stance, put the bat on your shoulder, look up at the sky, you notice a white fluffy cloud that reminds you of something you needed to do today. Suddenly here comes the pitch, but instead of a 90 mile per hour fastball, sinker, or slider, that you may be able to hit IF you were ready, it's a slow lumbering marshmallow that you could hit into the next state! It's what you've always wanted, what you've always dreamed of. However, you're standing there, weight on one leg, bat on your shoulder, by the time you're in hitting position...WOOSH...it's by you, and you only get ONE PITCH, but they didn't tell you that when you stepped up to the plate!

Waiting for that "Right" person to come into your life, is just like waiting at the plate for that one pitch, and it very rarely comes when you're fully prepared, and ready!

Sometimes the more prepared you are, the longer you have to wait, the Universe is very "Sneaky" about these things, it almost like it's

"Amusing" itself, messing with you.

So, what do you do in the game of "Ask & Receive" with the Universe. Before we get way to the philosophical realm here, if you want to adopt an M.O. keep these three letters in mind. A B R = Always Be Ready. You go to a singles bar, sure you're ready to meet someone, that's why you're there, you join a singles club, sure you're ready, that's the point.

You walk in to your local sports chain store to get something for your favorite sport. You've been playing your favorite sport, you're all sweaty, hair is a mess (should'a combed it in the car) one shoe is untied, and he/she (who's everything you've ever wanted as far as looks) walks up to you and says, "Do you have the time?", and you say..."Uh, I uh, I think it's uh, I'm not sure because I left my watch in the car"...or something like that.

INSTEAD OF: "*I think it's time I asked you if you are involved seriously with someone.*

Later after she/he walks away is when you think of that exact line, and that's when you tell yourself ALWAYS BE READY...YOU IDIOT!

One pitch, that's all you may get!

If someone challenged you to a contest in a sport you've never played, and they were an expert, would you bet on yourself? Would you step into the ring with an accomplished boxer if you've never had a fight? Boxing is not something you would want to learn by experience only, you would probably hit the canvas more than your opponent. You need advance "Training", and this is what we mean by "Being ready".

This "Being ready" thing, is the same type of "Contest", between you and Fait. You've got to come up with...not "Lines", because that can be phony and, sound like it's obviously been rehearsed, but intelligent responses. These are several rebuttals to spontaneous situations that have a high chance of occurrence. Practice delivering these rebuttals in a slight "Stammering" manner, to ad realism to the delivery, don't be so polished that it sounds like you've been rehearsing them over and over again.

In this case we're probably talking to the MEN

who are reading this, because they are more the "Pursuers" in the Man/Woman interaction, and more involved in the initial contact or "Opening lines", of a first meeting with the opposite sex. But those are only "Openers", and it's what you do AFTER the first "Opener" has been dropped, that really makes the difference. If the girl shows an interest by their actions (not walking away, or getting out their pepper spray) then it's time to proceed on to trying to find some common ground, like "I see you like XX's, or how do you like your new Chevy/Mazda, or whatever. Not, "Did it hurt...when you fell from Heaven"? Now that's a LINE! It's got to be a valid or legitimate question, or it is saying, "I'm just trying to find a reason to talk to you", which in some instances that's all it takes, so just do it! Now if you happen to be blessed with incredible looks, and are getting out of a high level sports car, then it doesn't really matter how stupid a line you come up with, but if this was your situation, you probably wouldn't be reading this book to begin with.

STORY:

A Man walks into a restaurant, sits down at the bar next to a very attractive woman, he smiles to let her know he acknowledges her presence, then orders a drink. He never tries to make conversation with her for 10 or 15 minutes. Then SHE starts the conversation, something to do with...anything...and they start talking. He never asks her about what she "Does" or where she's from or even what her name is, and never introduces himself. Now he's just created a "Hey, we're just all friends, bar buddies here", type of atmosphere.

Meanwhile he has just created aura of "Mystery" about him, because she's never encountered someone who in the first 5 minutes, hasn't tried to "Cozy up", to her, learn who she is, what she does, and tell her how great they are. He doesn't even want to learn her name (she thinks), it starts to worry her in the fact that her "Magic" might not work on this guy, or he's not too pressed to find someone, and he's not in the least bit, "Needy". Meanwhile, he's having a great time talking to people around him, watching the sports on TV, she is definitely not the center of his attention.

She is starting to get very attracted to this person who doesn't *NEED* her, but would still enjoy her presence, and maybe going a step further. Now when he initiates conversation with her, she is much more receptive, and finally he introduces himself, which takes the conversation to a more intimate level, and the situation gets more positive from that point on.

Did you ever have something in your hand, set it down somewhere and now you can't find it? You look and look, and can't figure out where you put it. So finally you quit looking thinking, "Oh it will turn up eventually" and then there it is right in front of you. The harder you look for it the harder it is to find. That example can be applied to "Finding" that special person. The harder you "Look" for that special someone, the harder it seems they are to find. Then when you give up looking, and just relax, there they are!

Opportunity seems to come along when you're least ready for it, so…ABR, (Always be ready). Don't go out to public places (grocery store, car wash, sporting event) looking like you slept in your clothes, need grooming, and are not at your best. Fate likes to "Play" with you, and sometimes waits until you're not projecting your best image, and that's when it throws you this "Fast ball" of opportunity. It's probably happened to you at least once, but did you learn from it? You probably wouldn't be reading this if you did!

As mentioned before, "Chance favors preparation", and this is no exception. The title of this chapter is "Are you ready" and that's the question you should always be asking yourself when you go out in public. You never know when that "Person of opportunity" will come along, so once again…ALWAYS BE READY…to make that "First impression."

CHAPTER 20

GOAL SETTING

Once again, if you don't know where you're going, how do you know when you get there?

Most people have never thought very much about setting an actual goal when it comes to finding a mate, partner, or even a potential mate or partner. They're like the proverbial leaf floating down the river, going wherever the wind and current takes them. If they come across someone who doesn't reject them, they think, "Wow this is great, now I've got a boy/girl friend. They are employing the "Learn by experience" method of finding someone to spend their time, or life with, and we all know about the Experience Axiom, right?

EXPERIENCE AXIOM:

Good judgment comes from experience, and a lot of that comes from bad judgment.

This can be very costly in wasted time, and effort, not to mention emotional stress and trauma. You have to decide several things in goal setting, and one of them is TAKING

ACTION. Once you realize that being PRO active is better that being RE active then you're on your way to changing your future, and materializing those goals. It doesn't matter if you're looking for a mate, lover, friend, even a business partner, YOU are the determining factor in making it happen. The sooner you realize that fact, the sooner you begin to take control of your life, and MAKE things happen (giving you more control) instead of waiting for things to happen (having less control).

If you want to attract someone of a higher level than you've been attracting, BE a person on a higher level than you are now. Once again, "You attract what you are".

If you are not familiar with goal setting then let us talk about the thought path necessary to make it happen.

Your mind is the world's most powerful computer, that when programmed with the correct data and can deliver very predictable results, guiding your life in the direction that is beneficial. One of the ways a person programs this computer is to give it a goal to achieve and a realistic time frame in which to accomplish this goal.

The problem with this powerful computer is, that once given this goal, it WILL complete this goal without any special instructions from its owner. I say "Problem" because if the programming is wrong, negative, or incorrect, that is JUST what you are going to get, negative results. It is this very situation that affects more people in a negative manner than a positive manner. Why? It's because the majority of people in everyday life have a negative based reality. They say things like, "Why do I screw things up, just when I'm doing so well", or "Why do I have to say the stupidest things when I don't know what to say?" You'll also hear them talking to themselves, "You are such an idiot", or "If I had a brain I'd be dangerous", all of this is negative programming. Your internal computer hears this, locks it in to it's formatting, and there you go down the long dark tube called the black hole of negativity into the pit of self-destruction and degradation.

The worse part about all this is, that it's a spiral that just keeps going down, getting worse at a faster rate. The more negative results you get, the more you comment on how this happens all the time, which produces more and worse negative results, and now you need a photograph of daylight just to remember what it looks like.

GOALS! They are the road map and catalyst of positive reprogramming.

This is why we have goal setting, because it is what programs this unrelenting computer in a POSITIVE manner.

Many people have asked me, "How DO you program this computer to give you positive results?" There is a very good quote from a British politician Dennis Healey who said, ***"When you find yourself in a hole, stop digging!"*** and I think that illustrates the thought pattern here.

First of all, in learning to reprogram your mental computer in positive manner with positive goals, you've got to learn how to QUIT programming it with negative input, (stop digging). So, how do you do that?

LISTEN

Listen to yourself more objectively when you talk to yourself. What do you say, and how do you say it?

Self-realization is a very difficult thing to accomplish, because you have to step outside of yourself to do it and...YOU'RE BIASED!

If you knew where your problems were, you'd probably correct them on your own, so in order to CORRECT these problems, you have to realize they exist; this is the "Stop digging" portion of the exercise.

Stop negative programming of your computer by **eliminating** any self-talk all together. Then you can start re-programming in a positive manner.

If you have an unsuccessful meeting or date with a member of the opposite sex, first of all don't automatically take the attitude that it was all your fault that you didn't hit it off. There are always factors beyond your control that can produce end results that are not pleasing.

In order to set a goal for yourself you need to

know where you could have done things differently, or more positively. Look back on the situation with a more objective eye, retrace your steps and at least make one goal. And that is to REMEMBER what happened with more clarity so that next time you can have a better recollection of the entire event.

So many people don't even know where they went wrong, what they did to turn the other person off, so you need to be able to recall the event as accurately as possible. In this case we are talking to the men here, because of what we will call the,

"Men/Women attraction Axiom".

Men will turn off Women far more often with their behavior than women will turn off men.

This is because of something women can give to men called...S E X, and if you haven't figured that out by now guys...you need this book more than you thought.

When you're a woman that's not grossly over weight, a minimum amount of facial hair and or scars, tattoos, braided armpits, and took a shower last week...you're a catch to most guys. There's very little you can to render yourself undesirable!

For both sexes: Still keep your mental recorder running all the time, and make a few mental notes as you go. What did we talk about that seemed to make her/him more attentive, and what things seemed to put him/her at a distance. Then you can begin to see where you may have said something, did something, or acted in a way to put the other person ill at ease. Now make it your goal to recognize this trait in someone, or some part of the conversation, and handle it in a more tactful manner.

EXAMPLE: If it's a first encounter, "Did I have to ask her/him their name more that once. Once again, the girl can forget the guy's name "Umpteen" times, but the guy gets only one chance, then he's branded as an empty headed "Neanderthal" who probably doesn't have a decent job, car, or apartment, and suddenly she sees someone she's just *got* to talk to.

Now your #1 goal as a guy is: **REMEMBER**

HER NAME! This is not rocket science. The hard part is remembering to *remember* to do it. People who always say, "I'm just really bad with names", should say they just really don't CARE what your name is. If I said to someone, before I told them my name, "I'll give you a hundred dollar bill if you can remember my name for 30 minutes." I guarantee you they would remember it. Why? Because it would be IMPORTANT to them. If you want to remember someone's name, make it important to you. Start practicing on everyone you meet not just some hot chick you want to get to know. When someone tells you their name, repeat it in your mind 10 times over and over again while you're talking to them. Then use it in a sentence in normal conversation. But, never let the conversation go 10 words past you recalling and *mentally* saying their name to yourself. You may even want to make up a visual picture of their name. Example: Mike = picture of a microphone and you making an announcement with it. Bob=Picture of you bobbing for apples at a Halloween party. Make up your own visualization but JUST DO IT!

STORY

BLIND DATE (From Chap. 7)

This is a re-cap of the earlier chapter talking about my friend at work and a girl I thought he would be compatible with. I think it's important enough to say a little more about it in GOAL SETTING. She was a nice girl, attractive, stable job, good academic background. I thought he was pretty much on the same level as related to the station of life, academic background, job level etc., as this girl. I mentioned to him that I had this female friend that he might enjoy meeting. He agreed and they got together on this blind date. Later I saw him at work and asked how things went. He said, "Wow she was really cute, didn't smoke, seemed intelligent, but she really talks a lot", trying to sugar coat the actual negative portion of the encounter. Finally he said, "She just goes on and on, I couldn't get a word in edgewise!"

This was a case of the woman turning the man off, and as previously mentioned RARELY ever happens. Men are not easy to turn off or be given cause to run from you if you are a woman of "Reasonable" attractiveness, and even have the most average level of personality.

In this case the girl should make one of her goals:

DON'T CONTINUEALLY DOMINATE THE CONVERSATION.

Which is something both sexes should have as a goal, because everyone wants to talk about themselves to try and impress the other person, make them feel as if they're out with Mr. Big or Ms. Princess. So goals are what we need to reprogram this super computer called our SUBCONSCIOUS MIND. You can make up some of these goals of our own, using your own personality as parameters. Write them down and put them in a central place where you see them all the time, like your bathroom mirror or kitchen table. Since they are rather private, keep them private when other people are around. But, just incase you can't think of any at the moment here's one that will turn any encounter into a positive one.

ASK MORE QUESTIONS ABOUT THE OTHER PERSON THAN YOU TALK ABOUT YOURSELF.

If you do this, it's almost a guaranteed end result that this person you're interacting with, will remember you in a positive manner, for a longer period of time than usual.

Why? Because very few people do that kind of thing when it comes to getting to know someone for the first time. Their main goal is to impress the other person, especially if that person is what they consider a little bit above their station in life, such as slightly better on the "Cute meter", better job, possessions, life style, and they feel like they need to come up to that perceived level of accomplishment.

CHAPTER 21

REJECTING THE WRONG PERSON

Have you ever known a couple who seem to be at odds with each other all the time, they're always arguing, there's always a crisis in their life that only one of them realizes as a crisis and the other thinks is nothing? They make you constantly ask yourself the question, "What DO they see in each other"? You can't imagine what pleasure they can take in being together, because you never see them in any kind of a pleasurable situation.

Somehow, some way, these two need each other, they feed off each other, and they obviously have been at it for some time.

You have to ask yourself, what brought them together to begin with, what do they see in each other and why do they stay together?

Unless you could enter each person's mind and actually BE that person, you'll never know the answer to that question, but how does it relate to you? You can take a lesson from these people, and ask how compatible do I want to be with that special someone, is this what I want, to be at odds all the time? Or do I want to have harmony in my life, intimacy and a loving attitude.

This is directed more to women, because the men are more the pursuers than the pursued, and so women have more "Opportunities" in dating with several men asking them out, interacting initially, and probably more first time encounters than their male counterparts.

Basically women get "Hit on" several times a day, especially if they're attractive. So how do you make the decision to go out with someone who you don't know very well or at all? How do you say "Yes" to having coffee, lunch, a first date, dinner and a movie, coming "UP" for a nightcap, and all the rest of the things that accompany that scenario?

It is a series of plateaus, each one getting higher on the level of knowledge about the other person, and also a level of intimacy, and comfort with just being with the other person.

Let's approach this with the idea that it is somehow easier to know what you DON'T want in someone, than what you DO want.

It's more important to recognize the WRONG person when they come into your life, and when you think about it, somewhat easier to see. The question for you is this. How SOON can you recognize that this is the wrong person? How many years will it take, or months will it take? Some people are together for 25 or more years, have several GRANDCHILDREN, and suddenly realize, "Hey, this is just not working out for us." Why did it take so long to realize this?

Maybe they realized it after the 2nd child was born, and now they have to stay together "For the children". Now the kids have moved out, and they need to stay together because it's too late to "Start over", and so we'll just tolerate each other rather that split up.

All of these scenarios play out every day in the lives of many people, because they didn't recognize the fact that something just was not "Right" in the relationship on the 2nd or 3rd date, but the physical attraction overpowered their common sense.

As previously stated: ***EMOTION TRUMPS COMMON SENSE EVERY TIME.***

Once again it comes under the heading of being PROactive instead of Reactive. If you want your life to go in a certain direction, MAKE it go in that direction and don't settle for less thinking, "This is the best I'm going to get."

TRUTH: The more you use your 6th sense or intuition the stronger it becomes.

If something or someone doesn't "Feel" right, then it's not right, don't ignore it. What is being said here is very simple, the less time it takes you to realize you are cultivating a relationship with the wrong person, the more successful you can become in finding the right person.

Once again it comes under the heading of know where the train tracks go first, and if you don't like the answer, don't get on the train, because that's where you're going to end up.

STORY

The Anchor

Once upon a time there was a man who owned a beautiful sailboat, it had everything on it to make your sailing experience the most fun, and enjoyable time possible. It also had an anchor and because the man wanted the boat to look first class he had the anchor gold plated, and polished to a bright sparkling shine. He loved his boat and also this very unique piece of hardware. He was anchored one day near a beautiful island where the water was rather shallow about 20 feet all the way to shore. The winds came up and blew the boat into one of the coral shoals about 100 yards from shore and the boat began to sink and go down. The man loved his anchor so much and didn't want it to drop over a deep abyss just off shore, so he dove down and caught it and began to drag it to shore. He was getting more tired and running out of air in his lungs, but he thought "I can make it just a little further." As he drug the anchor along the bottom he thought he could make it, and so held on to the anchor getting more and more tired. The longer he held on to the anchor the less air he had and more tired he became, until at the last minute he let go of the anchor and tried to swim to the surface. He didn't make it. He gulped in water, it filled his lungs and he drowned. He held on to the anchor a bit too long.

All of the people in the previous scenarios had a different kind of "Anchor" and how long did they carry it before deciding, "If I don't let go, I'm going to *go down with the ship*", so to speak.

The question here is, what (or who) is your anchor, and how long will it take you to let go of it (or them).

It's up to you to realize in your relationships, "Do I have an anchor, or a life boat", and realize this quickly.

If you think you have an anchor already, ask yourself, "How long am I going to hold on to this thing before I decide to let go, and get on with my life?

Drop the Anchor

Once you've decided you have made a mistake, how long will it take you to drop the anchor of disharmony and separate yourself from that person who is causing you the problem by being the wrong person FOR YOU.

There once was an old Chinese guru who's words were regarded as advice to live by, and everyone wanted an audience with him. After waiting a very long time to speak with this all knowing sage, a young man asked him, "How do I break these chains of this habit I have of drinking, smoking, and wild living? Immediately the old man got up and walked over to a giant pillar that was holding up the temple, and grabbed it with all his might. He then said, "Oh please free me from this pillar, I can't take it any more, please set me free?" The young man replied, "You old fool, the pillar is not holding you it's the other way around, just let go of it?" The Master then replied, "Now you understand who is holding who in the fight to lose your unwanted habits. Instead of holding on so tight, just let go of them."

Don't let one wrong decision, or one mistake affect the rest of your life if you can do something about it. Remember:

THE PREDICTION AXIOM:

PAST PERFORMANCE OR EVENTS DO NOT GUARANTEE OR PREDICT FUTURE SUCCESS OR FAILURE

Which means, just because you made one mistake, missed one opportunity, or made one "Oops", in one area of your life, that doesn't mean you have to repeat it over and over again, OR in another area of your life. Example: So you lost a sporting contest in your favorite game or match to someone of lesser ability. That doesn't mean you're going to lose that big account at work, and get fired tomorrow. And just the opposite is true, just because you were victorious and WON that tennis/golf/volleyball trophy it doesn't mean you are going to be top salesperson of the month with out a lot of work, and success is just going to fall out of the blue into your lap.

Nor, just because you were "King of the mountain" for one event doesn't mean you can easily climb back up there any time you want and you're always going hit a home run when you get up to the "Plate of life."

Learning by your mistakes means REALIZING your mistakes as YOUR mistakes, not other people trying to trip you up, bad luck, just bad CHOICES, but they were YOUR choices.

You can't change the past, and the present is only the present for ONE SECOND, then it becomes the past. The only thing you can have the slightest chance of changing or altering is the FUTURE! But then again because it's in the future, you don't really know what is going to happen. You can project what you THINK is going to happen in the future and therein is the focus of directing our lives.

Each successful outcome in every area of our life is preceded by careful planning and a thing called WORK. Attracting or meeting just the right person for you is no different.

Using the past as a guide to shaping the future is what all of us TRY to do. The trouble is, maybe we are wearing "Refractory" Rose Colored glasses, that tend to improve the look of the situation at hand. They make it look more appealing because we think we need it. Or they mask out negative areas causing us to overlook the negative part because we want the positive part so much.

This is why people make bad, or "Wrong" decisions in life and choosing a mate, spouse, or significant other is one of those major decisions.

Learn to recognize the warning signs of "Impending relationship disaster".

Would you go sailing on a boat that you knew had a hole in the hull? Some people would, saying, "But it's such a beautiful boat, maybe we can fix that hole after we're at sea. "Those same people would probably do the same thing in a relationship saying, "Well, he/she has some emotional problems/baggage, but what a beautiful xxxx he/she's got.

10 WARNING SIGNS

What are some of the warning signs you've got the "Wrong" person on your hands?

1. They want to "Change" you

They are repeatedly telling you how you could be "Better" at what you're doing. How you could "Improve" your xxxx in several of the areas of your life. If they keep doing this over and over again, this should tell you something..."They're not satisfied with me the way I am." Run, don't walk away from this person.

2. You have more than 2 arguments a week, especially about trivial things.

3. They say the following when you go out to a party, etc. of THEIR friends...

"Is THAT what you're wearing?" Just another indication that they want you to look better, be better, and dress better that everyone else there, because you're with THEM! Goes back to wanting to change you.

4. They ask you, "Do you REALLY need another one of these? (Tennis racquet, golf clubs, shoes, dresses, hats, any thing else you enjoy having)

5. They tell you, "Sure I can quit drinking/smoking, any time I want. Do you really believe that enough to say "I do" at the

alter?

6. If you hear this once, run the other way: "It's your fault this happened!" When someone loves you unconditionally it doesn't matter who's fault it is that anything happened.

7. You hear this phrase from them, "I saw the way you looked at her/him." Jealousy has no place in a relationship where there is natural harmony. If you truly love & trust the other person, you're not worried that they are "Looking" to find someone else. Or have an interest in someone else.

8. "I need my own space", if you hear this you should put a LOT of space between you and person that told you this, and permanently. It's just their way of saying, "I don't want to be around you any more." Is that the kind of person you want to cling to, spend your life, or even another week with?

9. If they say, "I love animals more than I love people." Tell them to buy an extra dog or cat, because that's who they really belong with to be happy. You can't compete with "Fluffy" to make

them happy.

10. If their most repeated phrase is, "Why do you always have to _____. Nobody ALWAYS does anything. This is a person who has a skewed view of reality, and their perception gets blown out of proportion. They also say, "I've told you a 1000 times that _____ etc. You need to reply with, "I'm only going to say this once...GOODBYE!

These are just guidelines to give you a better feel of how people relate to problems, and others around them. Use this information to evaluate someone you "Think" you may be interested in, and if it gives you the smallest hint of a problem, then that problem will become bigger as the days, months, or if you let it happen...years go buy.

THE SANDPAPER SYNDROME

Take a piece of sandpaper and rub it back and forth across your knuckle. Doesn't hurt too much - right away does it? Do it some more, and it becomes a little irritating. Keep doing it and when the top layer of skin comes away, you're in downright pain! That's the way you could view things that irritate you in a relationship. The other person has a habit you think you can live with, and you try to overlook it, but as time goes on it becomes harder to ignore. You're thinking if they know this irritates you, why do they continue to do it? So when you mention it to them they think it's such a small problem that they continue to do it. The phrase, "Little things become big things", begins to pop up in your mind, and you're asking yourself, "If they care so much about me why can't they change or correct this behavior." Now you begin to question how much do they care about you. The little things have just grown a dragon's head, claws, and a tail, because they REPRESENT a *value system* that you are now beginning to question. Do they love you or not? This is not rocket science, this finally becomes the big question in the end...how much do you care for me, if you keep doing the things I've already told you that I don't like?

Look for the warning signs, when you see any one of them, it may be time for a serious REevaluation of your relationships.

CHAPTER 22

IS IT WRITTEN IN THE STARS?

This is not a book about astrology but there is a germ of truth in the school of thought that whatever "Star" you were born under has a relation to the person you are best suited for.

When does life become life? How does it develop? Why are you ... you? Have you been here before? What is the scheme of things, why don't we know the answers to these and many other bewildering questions? Where did it all start? What about a supreme power that caused it all to begin? If God created it all, where did God come from? You could go on forever about the chicken and the egg thing, so let's just skip all that and jump right up to the time called NOW.

Let's start with the gravitational pull of the stars on a developing embryo. DNA chromosomal make-up is the soup that nature stirs up when creating human characteristics and personality traits. Let's assume certain genes are brought to the surface as the results of a certain degree of gravitational pull by the planets, stars and moon. I don't know how much of this I believe, but I do know each person born in a certain time of the year tends to have many of same personality traits associated with that astrological sign. Taurus people are supposed to be truthful, bull headed, loyal to only few, and like music and art. I'm a Taurus and I can't tell a lie, it's too much trouble to remember what I said. I feel my way is the right way, only have 3 close friends, and have been a professional guitar player/vocalist with an AA degree in commercial art and a BS in art education. Formerly a high school art teacher, I spent 22 years as a graphic artist/designer draftsman for a large construction corporation. If you look at my personality profile and compare it with Taurus traits you have to give the stars some credence, because I have every one of those characteristics.

OK, so maybe Astrology has some relationship to our lives, but how can this help us? It illustrates the fact that there are unseen forces out there that can help us or hurt us. The main thing to focus upon is, that you have certain personality traits - don't fight it, let it help you. Go with the flow of energy you were given to help you. For instance, if you're not good at lying, don't become a salesman. Not that all salespeople are liars, but I've never met a good salesperson yet that told the complete truth. The truth about truth is; no one really wants to hear it. It's boring. It's the way life really is, usually blah, and it doesn't sell houses, cars, stocks, investments, and other items, that are also boring, but needed.

That's why people who sell drugs, hookers, and porno, are never out of work and have more business than they can handle...it's NOT boring. It's another reason people who write and try to sell self-improvement books, (like this) are not on the top of the N.Y. best seller list, because most people don't feel they **need** improvement. They think they're fine just the way they are, living in their car, sticking a needle in between their toes because they don't want track marks on their arms, and prostituting themselves in all kinds of ways, just to get out of the many kinds of trouble they've put themselves in initially.

You sell the sizzle not the steak, and sizzle does not always parallel the truth!

You were created with a certain mold, and have certain characteristics and traits. Learn what these are, and capitalize upon them, don't go against them. Below are the twelve months of the Zodiac, and the personality characteristics (according to Astrologers) that go with them. See where you fall and how close your actual traits match the list. Learn some of the other Astrological signs, and their characteristics, it will help you get to know people better and may give you an insight into their world of reference. Look at it this way: even if you think it's all hogwash, at least you'll have something interesting to talk about at a party.

PERSONALITY TRAITS OF DIFFERENT ZODIAC SIGNS:

Aries: People falling under this sign are adventurous. They are generally self-willed and courageous. They may be seen as short-tempered individuals. They are often clever and confident. On some occasions they act impatiently. Their impulsiveness and quick temper can be their potential enemies. If they overcome these weaknesses, they can achieve success in life, owing to their confidence and clarity in thinking.

Taurus: Those belonging to this sign are romantics. Their love for style and beauty is apparent in their way of living. They are warm at heart and prefer being secure in life. As friends, they are trustworthy and helpful. But they can be possessive about everything they have. This may translate to selfishness and greed. If on guard about these negativities, a Taurus can make good company and an excellent friend. COMPATIBLE: Cancer, Virgo, Capricorn, Pisces

Gemini: People belonging to this sign are versatile and quick-witted. They are spontaneous in communication. They come across as intelligent people. Their love towards life is evident from their living! But they tend to worry too much on certain issues and fail in managing their stress. They form opinions pretty quickly and sometimes appear to look superficially at life.

Cancer: Those falling under this zodiac sign form the sentimental lot. They are a group comprised of a loving and caring nature. They are cautious in their actions. They are very protective towards their loved ones. This nature makes them excellent and caring parents. Cancers often have an imaginative and artistic side to their life. They are subject to varying moods. Their overly emotional nature needs to be worked on. On the whole, they are good human beings.

Leo: Leos are generous, open-minded, and are quite caring. They possess a dominating nature coupled with a knack of taking everyone along. This combination of traits make them true leaders. They may be egotistic and bossy. They tend to easily lose their temper. They are both open-minded and openhanded, and show deep love for magnificence and luxury. Leos are real kings!

Virgo: They are very analytical. They tend to think overly on any given subject and base their conclusions on a long thought process and deep analysis. They have unidirectional talents. They are absolute purists. Their overcritical nature can become a cause of their troubles but otherwise they are intelligent and good decision-makers.

Libra: Their romantic nature is coupled with serenity. They are balanced in nature and know how to keep their cool at all occasions. At times, they find it difficult to express themselves. Though they appear aloof, they are attached to their near ones. They tend to get influenced by the views of others. It makes them indecisive. Apart from these faults, they are on the whole reasonable and thoughtful.

Scorpio: Scorpios are passionate individuals with a magnetic personality. They are forceful about going by their opinions. They have clarity of thought and expression. Due to their possessive nature, they become jealous quite easily. They are clever and courageous. They can be resentful and obsessive. They seek to take revenge of the wrongdoers. So be careful while dealing with Scorpios.

Sagittarius: They are intelligent and philosophical. They know how to lighten up any atmosphere. They are fun-loving in nature.

Sometimes their excessive optimism makes them behave carelessly. Their moods and whims can be bothersome but on the whole, they are intelligent people with a good sense of humor.

Capricorn: They are prudent and practical. Their ambitious nature does not allow them to ever give up. They are vigilant. They plan before playing any game of life. They may come across as sadistic individuals who are orthodox and rigid. Perseverance and tolerance are their greatest qualities. They are generally upfront in fighting whatever comes in their way.

Aquarius: They are among the intelligent in the crowd. A sense of humor, coupled with great intelligence and deep thinking make them stand out. They make loyal and honest friends. They are independent thinkers with great originality in their thoughts and actions. They may appear indifferent and less emotional. If you have an Aquarian around you, you may find it difficult to understand him/her.

Pisces: They are sensitive and sympathetic. They are kind and helpful. They can go out of their way to help their dear ones. This makes them excellent friends. Opinions of others can easily influence them due to which they can easily get carried away. They are not very determined or courageous. They are often vague in thinking and behavior. But their idealism is their true differentiator.

Zodiac Sign Compatible Signs Incompatible Signs

Zodiac Sign	Compatible Signs	Incompatible Signs
Aries (March 21 to April 19)	Gemini, Leo, Sagittarius, Aquarius	Cancer, Capricorn, Libra
Taurus (April 20 to May 20)	Cancer, Virgo, Capricorn, Pisces	Leo, Aquarius, Scorpio
Gemini (May 21 to June 20)	Libra, Aquarius, Aries, Leo	Virgo, Pisces, Sagittarius
Cancer (June 21 to July 22)	Taurus, Virgo, Scorpio, Pisces	Aries, Libra, Capricorn
Leo (July 23 to August 22)	Aries, Gemini, Libra, Sagittarius	Taurus, Scorpio, Aquarius
Virgo (August 23 to September 22)	Taurus, Cancer, Scorpio, Capricorn	Gemini, Sagittarius, Pisces
Libra (September 23 to October 22)	Gemini, Leo, Sagittarius, Aquarius	Cancer, Capricorn, Aries
Scorpio (October 23 to November 21)	Cancer, Virgo, Capricorn, Pisces	Leo, Aquarius, Taurus
Sagittarius (November 22 to December 21)	Aries, Leo, Libra, Aquarius	Virgo, Pisces, Gemini
Capricorn (December 22 to January 19)	Taurus, Virgo, Scorpio, Pisces	Aries, Libra, Cancer
Aquarius (January 20 to February 18)	Aries, Gemini, Libra, Sagittarius	Scorpio, Taurus, Leo
Pisces (February 19 to March 20)	Taurus, Cancer, Scorpio, Capricorn	Gemini, Sagittarius, Virgo

Keep in mind that these signs and the information that they convey should not be taken as the "Last word" in direction when evaluating a potential mate, partner, or friend. They are just to be used as a general measuring stick to cast further light on the bewildering dilemma of recognizing your Mr./Ms. Right from Mr./Ms. Wrong, in hopes of pointing you in the right direction and influencing your choices.

Once again success in anything you do, let alone, LIFE, is all about choices, and the more irreversible a choice is, the more it had better be the right one.

Regard this chart as "More information", to help you in making choices related to aligning yourself to another member of the opposite sex. The more information you can get on any subject to make a decision, the better chance you have in making the right choice.

CHAPTER 23

THE "KITTY" SYNDROME

So now you have met someone you feel "Good" about, and you're getting comfortable with them, you're probably wondering "How do I hold on to them?" How do you keep the attraction still attractive, to the point of drawing that other person closer to you without holding too tight.

There is a phenomena I call the "Kitty syndrome", and it illustrates the problem many people have when meeting someone that they really like, feel like this person is something special, and would like it to be more than it already is, sometimes before it's ready to be that.

You know how cats are, right? They're independent, do what they want when they want, sleep when they want, and under no circumstances will come when called if they don't feel like coming. They like to be stroked and petted, when THEY feel like getting stroked and petted. They even like to held once in a while. So now you're holding Kitty in your arms and she is half asleep, dozing off, she's purring and things are very peaceful. Suddenly Kitty wakes up and her little cat brain thinks of something she's just got to do, and she wants down. You, however are not done with the petting, and stroking, and holding, so you hold on to Kitty. Kitty is now more determined to get down, and begins to let you know...*RAHGNER, SPITTSZ-Pfffttt,hiss*, and a few other cat words you don't understand, and you can't understand why Kitty doesn't like this petting thing anymore, so you hold on to her. The more you hold on, the stronger (you didn't know a cat could be this strong) and wilder Kitty seems to get, and POW...Kitty is flying through the air toward the floor, and you have these big scratches and bite marks all over your arms.

This is just an example of how some people are in a relationship when they decide they want more of the other person's time, affection, love, and whatever. The quickest way to end a relationship is holding on too tight, and the other person is going to react just exactly like

"Kitty" and the more you hold on, the more they are going to draw back. Your behavior is going to cause them to want "More space" and look at you as a controller type of person that they have got to get away from. That's when they give you that, "It's not you it's me"...line.

If you really want to keep someone interested in you, the best thing to do is to give them the space in their life to be themselves, do their own thing, whatever that is, while still letting them know you do care a great deal about them, their problems, and desires. This type of attitude will go a very long way in cementing a relationship with someone, because it's not everyday that someone experiences this open type of freedom giving the other person this leeway. In every relationship there is usually one person who needs more reassurance, more attention, and more assurance that they are being "Wanted", or appreciated. If you want natural harmony in your relationships with people remember this:

FREEDOM AXIOM: *THE ONLY HOLD YOU HAVE OVER SOMEONE IS WHAT THEY GIVE YOU.*

That in it self produces an Oxymoron, (A figure of speech in which contradictory terms appear in conjunction with each other, EXAMPLE: vegetarian meatloaf) this is to say that you have a "Hold" over someone because you are **not** holding them. At any rate, the more freedom you give someone the more you bind them to you. This is especially true when several of their recent relationships were with people who tried to control them and their belief systems. Remember the "Kitty syndrome". Don't hold the "Kitty" too tight or you will find bite marks and scratches all over your "Heart", not to mention your ego.

CHAPTER 24

VALUE SYSTEMS

You may have heard the saying, "One man's ceiling is another man's floor", it's also a song by Paul Simon. Essentially it is saying that no matter who you are, there is always someone above you, or waiting to take your place if you fail.

This is somewhat the same phenomena in dating, the pursuit of women by men, men by women, the pursuit of anyone in our society who's trying to climb the ladder of success. We all want something better than we've got, or something better than we are. Yes, better than we ARE, better looking than we are, more successful financially than we are, smarter than we are, and of course YOUNGER that we are.

In a highly rated sitcom there is a loveable loser who just can't seem to make the right choice, can't pick the right horse, meet the "Right" girl, and is thoroughly content with being the worlds worst loser at everything and anything. With women is favorite saying is, "When I like them, they don't like me, and when they like me, I don't like them."

That pretty well sums it up for thousands of people who are out there searching for that perfect girlfriend/boyfriend or mate, and let's ask the question...why?

Picture this illustration. You're standing on a cliff, just across a small cavern there is another cliff just above you and one just below you. On the one above you there is a very attractive member of the opposite sex, and maybe even more attractive than you. On the other ledge below you, there is a "Lesser attractive than you", member of the opposite sex. It appears that the assent to the cliff above you is much more difficult and dangerous than the one below you. You try to get the attention of that person above you but you can't because they are trying to get the attention of the person on the next cliff just above them.

The person on the cliff below you is trying to get your attention to "Come on down", but they can't because you're focused on that person on the cliff above you.

Each person is always looking for that "Step up"

when it comes to looks, and material values. We all want more than we're worth, better than we deserve, and then when we get it we find out how much trouble it is to maintain, and complain about how now we have to work harder to keep this status quo.

Why is this?

It's because of a little thing called "Value systems", and each person has a different set of values, and a slightly different value system. Some people have a value system that is very close to their friends' values, because people tend to attract others like themselves with their ideas and values.

When you begin to evaluate a potential relationship based on values, instead of just outward appearance or as most of us say, LOOKS, then you begin to realize what natural harmony between two people is all about. When you begin to alter your "Rating system" to encompass more than just looks, you begin to allow yourself to open the choices that were there all along but you couldn't see them because you were only focusing on one little area of attraction.

Some of these criteria of values might be:

1. How close are this person's values and ideas to my own?

2. What are their talents compared to mine?

3. What is their level of intensity and passion compared to mine?

4. How credible/truthful are they in what they proclaim to be important?

5. How unwavering are they in their beliefs?

6. How opinionated are they compared to my ideas?

Make up your own criteria of evaluation for this "Special" person you're looking for, and apply it to everyone you meet, just to get in "Practice" using it on the object of your affection. It will suddenly open up a new world of understanding just by the ACT of trying to learn more about people in general.

If nothing else it will teach you how to ASK QUESTIONS of other people without appearing too inquisitive. This is called the art of communication, and it's something very few people have gotten to first base on, let alone mastered.

When you begin to learn about someone's values and what they think is important, then you start to gain a better and higher "Vision" of that person. You also begin to learn a little bit about their level of intelligence, background, upbringing, personal history, and you have a deeper understanding of why they do the things they do, and react to stimuli in the way that displays their outward behavior.

In an earlier chapter I wrote about a comparison of being able to rise high up above the ground to be able to see where a set of train tracks went miles beyond the boarding station. Life is a little like getting on a train at the station and not having a schedule, you have no idea of where that train is going to take you. But, if you could rise high in the air above the horizon and see where the tracks went, who needs a schedule?

Finding out a person's belief system, or value system is a little like being able to see where the tracks of that person's "Train" are going BEFORE you get on. It's an indication of what the ride will be like, and if you don't like where the tracks go, is there any reason the train will arrive at a different place when it pulls into the station?

It may be a great Bullet Train, with a beautiful dinning car, award winning chef, have a great club car with live music ...but If you don't like where the tracks go, you won't like where you'll end up. Don't get on *that* train, or at least have enough sense to get off at the next stop...if there is one!

Value systems give you a higher level of predicting another person's future achievements, and or failures. They give "Predictability" to a relationship and illustrate the probability of the success or failure of that relationship.

OLD ENGLISH PROVERB: If you spend time watering a lemon tree, don't expect to get peaches. The time you spend with someone is like watering that tree, make sure it's going to give you the fruit you love, then...**JUST DO IT!**

CHAPTER 25

TRYTH & LIES

KNOW WHEN YOU'RE BEING LIED TO

When people meet each other for the first time they try to impress each other, right? You want to make yourself look bigger, better, brighter, smarter, funnier, prettier, more creative and we could go on forever. It's a wonder anybody learns anything about anyone, because each person is telling, telling, talking about how great they did this or that, when they were this or that. How much of that blah blah do you think is real anyway?

Truth is a simple concept, right? If that's the "Truth" why are so many people not employing the truth all the time, 50% of the time, 10% of the time or any of the time?

Some people never tell the truth, they would rather tell a "Fib" or fabrication of the event than what really happened, because it's soooo, much more interesting that the truth. It's easy to spot these people, because they always have a "Better story" that you just told. They can never tell the truth because their lives don't have any "Pizzazz" to it, they've always been the low man/woman on the "Totem pole of life" and the only way they and feel better or good about themselves is to fabricate some information about what they "Did" last night, or last week, or last year, or when they were a "King" in high school. A good indicator of how much they have got going for them in their PRESENT life, is how far back they have to go to get a "Story" that they feel you will regard as "Interesting", or that rivals the experience you just related. So…they fabricate one that's somewhat close to the truth, but if it were the truth it wouldn't be glamorous enough or interesting enough so it's something FAR from "The truth".

Wouldn't it be great if every time someone is telling a lie a red light popped up from behind them and started blinking? Or a little bell went off in their shirt pocket and you heard "Ding ding" which would tell you in an instant when someone was not telling the truth.

Guess what, there is such a thing. There is a little red light that goes off, but you have to be wearing "Special glasses" to see it. They are the glasses of NLP, or Neuro-linguistic Programming. This is a method devised by some psychologists that holds true in almost every culture, every national group and 98% of everyone you meet and talk to every day. This is something that you need to look up on the web, or anywhere there is a vast amount of info at your disposal. It tells you that when people use their brains to formulate or convey information that they are either receiving or transmitting, their EYES dart to specific areas of the space in front of them. Based on knowing what to look for when you see this eye position in someone, you will know in 90% of people you talk to, IF they're lying or not. Eye position is only a "Tip of the iceberg" in the non-verbal informational transference between people. There are several other factors that tell you a lot about someone's degree of truth or non-truth (which we will call a lie because it is not the WHOLE truth) by the position of their eyes when asked a question. If they are truly accessing their brain for information their eyes will go one of two places, either up to right or up to the left. The signal for RIGHT HANDED PEOPLE when they access their brain for information REMEMBERED, is up and to THEIR left or YOUR right when looking at them. Bottom line, if a RIGHT HANDED (Opposite for lefties) person is accessing their brain for information in the past, that's ALREADY happened or already exists, their eyes will go up and to YOUR right when facing them (their left). This is the signal that they are accessing information they already know as a fact, it's already happened, it's history, and usually the truth.

In contrast, if someone constructs a picture, or information like MAKING a picture they have never seen before, (a lie) their eyes (if they are right handed) will go up and to THEIR right, or your left when facing them. So if you say, "What would your house look like if it were painted shocking pink with black polka dots"? They've never seen this before so they have to "Construct" the picture, and their eyes will go up and to their right (your left).

So big deal, you're thinking, how does this help

me know if my boyfriend, girlfriend, wife, husband, business partner, etc., is lying?

A LESSON IN NLP

To over simplify the positions of someone's eyes when accessing their brain, and to teach you a little bit about NLP, and how your brain calls up information, there is a little diagram on the last page of this chapter. It tells you, in general, where a person's eyes will flash to (WHEN FACING YOU) when they are thinking of certain kinds of information:

Information Remembered-VSIUAL: the eyes will go up and to YOUR right. This would be their brain conveying information to them that they remembered, most likely it is the truth...because they are REMEMBERING it, the way it actually happened.

Information Constructed: Usually a lie, because they are "Making this up". The eyes would go up and to YOUR left. They are CONSTRUCTING the picture that they've never actually seen before, so it's a fabrication of something that never happened. Depending on their rate of speech (choppy and a lot of filler words like a lot of "Um's, and I-Ah's or verbal stumbling) you can get an idea of the degree of credibility and therefore truth of the information that you're hearing.

Audio (sounds) **Remembered:** The eyes would go level and to YOUR left. Example: "What's the sound of your mother's voice?" Trying to remember that would be remembering something that already EXISTED. Any time someone is telling you something they REMEMBERED, it's usually the truth.

AUDIO Information Constructed: The eyes would go level and to YOUR right. Example: How would your car sound without a muffler? You've never heard your car without a muffler so you would imagine or CONSTRUCT the sound you think it would sound like. Example: "How did you like that concert by XXX?" If someone has never heard that concert, but want to sound like they did because they think that will make you like them, and give them credibility, their eyes will go to YOUR right and they might say something like, "I, ah, thought it was ah, um, really ah.... great. Your response, "What part did you really like?". Their response,

"I ah, liked, ah, the whole thing in general." THEY'RE BUSTED!

Kinesthetic (Feelings) **Remembered:** The eyes would go down and to YOUR right: Example: "How did you feel when your cat got run over?"

Kinesthetic Constructed: Eyes down and to YOUR left. Ex: "How do you feel about that memo our new boss put out?" Since they've never read this memo but want to act like they did, the eyes may go down and to YOUR left, and the speech would sound much the same with filler words, and verbal stumbling plus generalizations. This would be a manufactured or constructed feeling that they just came up with, has no basis in reality. THEY'RE BUSTED!

These are just pointers in helping you get to know someone on a deeper level quicker, and cut through all the fodder and fluff that accompanies new relationships

The wife that knows her husband's every idiosyncrasy, and is attuned to all his in's and out's, she's lived with him for 30 years and knows when he's lying, how does she do it? She has subconsciously become attuned to each little detail of his eyes, breathing; skin coloring, and eye blink rate per second, and each body movement. When he's not telling the truth, his eyes go to a different position, his breathing increases, and his skin color around his cheeks turn a bright red. But, she does not CONSCIOUSLLY know that she knows this, she only knows he's lying. If she took a course in NLP she would "Know *why* she knows" this.

When a person is fabricating a piece of VISUAL info like "How would your car look painted red and yellow" their eyes will go up and to THEIR RIGHT which is YOUR left.

So if the wife says, "What'd you do last night when I was out of town?" And, his eyes go up and to the RIGHT (her left) and he says, "Oh, just got together with a bunch of the boys and played poker all night", that's the signal he is FABRICATING information he has not seen or experienced yet. A LIE! The wife immediately gets a, "This is hogwash" signal and instantly knows he's not telling the whole or any truth. Especially when he starts shuffling his feet, and adjusting his hat, because she's knows that type of behavior is consistent with HIS lying and the patterns associated with him in a lie.

It's so much easier to tell the truth, you don't have to remember what you lied about, because you've got the truth in your mind to go back to.

So, why do people lie? In business it's to gain an advantage, make more money, shift the blame to someone else, or steal someone's idea and make it look like their own. Who knows, there a hundred reasons why someone lies instead of telling the truth, but one thing is true, a lie weakens a person's position because EVENTUALLY it will be discovered, and then you will branded as "A LIER", which is not good! No one will trust you, you're a piece of kaka, a traitor to anyone who knows you and no body will ever believe you again. People look the other way when you come into the room, and avoid talking to you, all because you told a lie...ONCE!

How does this affect the person in question? Any lie you tell weakens your power to create good for yourself and those around you. Remember the most important truth, "THOUGHTS ARE THINGS" and when you lie or come up with non-truths, you are creating forces in the Universe that can become REAL and will invariably rob you of the power you had before. Before you know it you're going downhill on a flaming skateboard into a lake of gasoline!

Just stick to the truth, it's a lot easier to remember, people will not be so aggravated at you, and may lend you their support later when you need it.

In relationships, your mate, friend, or potential friend is going to get to know the "Real" you sooner or later. When they do, if the "Real you" is too big of a surprise, they're out the door. You're back at square one, telling yourself, "Next time it's going to be different." In the next diagram, these referrences are given as you are facing someone, so up to the rt. for you is opposite (up and to the left) for them. Look at it this way, when facing them, eyes up and to the right IS right (truth), to the left is fabrication (lie). BUT...it's all reversed for left handed people. **THAT IS IMPORTANT!**

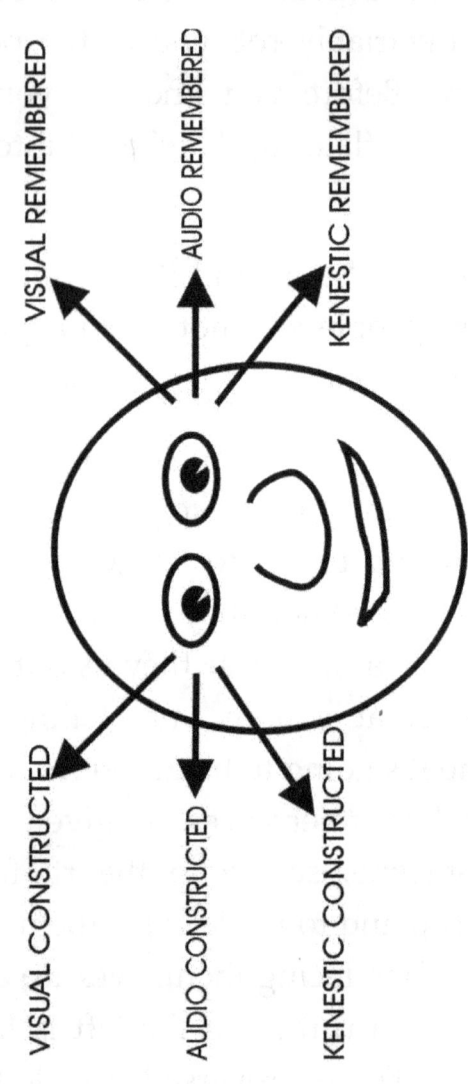

CHAPTER 26

PERSONALITY TYPES

Ask yourself, what actually makes people get along, become successful in relationships, and draw others TO them instead of repel others FROM them?

Why do you like someone in the first 60 seconds after meeting, and feel just the opposite about someone else in the same time frame? As long as there have been men and women this phenomena of attraction/repulsion has been a mystery for all who study it as well as experience it first hand.

What is it that draws you to someone beyond just physical appearance. Sure we all want that hunk of a movie actor type of guy, or that "Playmate of the month" type of girl, but then unless you're that kind of counter part, you know it will never happen with what you have to bring to the table. So...you settle into what we call, "Reality", and start looking for the best you can get with what you got to give. In this great all consuming search for "Mr. Right or Ms. perfect" you need to make the best of your time, because no matter how old you are...your clock is ticking. The funny thing about it is, the older you get the faster it ticks...it seems. With that in mind, let's explore an area of human development called "Personality types".

Some personality types fit together well, and then of course some don't. As you go through life you are witness to many "Square pegs", fitting into "Round holes", so to speak and you go away shaking your head thinking what do those two see in each other.

Let us examine some personality types and try to come up with somewhat of an answer to why it works (sometimes) and why not (sometimes). First of all what ARE the personality types.

In my 15 years of managing a singles club and being responsible for hundreds of introductions of members of the opposite sex, I have had the chance to come in contact with an ocean of people from all walks of life, and personality types. I've broken it down to several types of people who seem to share the same mannerisms, values, and desires. I've also watched how they all get along, or don't, and maybe these realizations are correct, maybe they're totally bogus, and just maybe they will help you in your quest of hunting for that "Just right" person. You make the call.

VALUE SCALES - MEN VS. WOMEN

Before we go into the personality types, we must understand some of the variables that can offset this illustration or picture of different personalities.

First of all let's look at this "Man/woman thing" of attraction in the full light of the term "Symbiotic". Which in this case means, each person does, or has something the other person wants, and doesn't mind giving it up for what they get, even though it's not what they REALLY want, or is their ideal answer to what they're searching for. In other words it's what they'll "Settle" for because they can't get what they really want. There are many degrees of "Settling" if we want to use that term for lack of a better one. If 100% is what we call perfect, then let's work downward from that.

Example: "Well, he's/she's 80% of what I've been looking for so I guess I can overlook 20%

of his/her faults or negativities."

This is a gross over simplification of what is trying to be conveyed, but you get the picture. Each person is different in their ability to adjust the "Automatic evaluator" inside their belief system, and they make these adjustments every day, hour and minute of their lives on every level, not only male/female interaction.

WOMEN

OK, let's face it, a woman has something a man wants and can't get anywhere else, which is the "Equipment" for a great sexual experience. No matter what she looks like, THIS is her barging "Tool", and some women are better "Negotiators" than others. The more she knows how to use this "Tool", and other female tools, the more and higher levels of men she can keep, once she gets them into her web of "Satisfaction" or a more general term, sphere of influence. In simpler terms, as long as she is not off the scale of unattractiveness, (over weight, disfigured, missing limbs, single with 5 kids) this "Tool" can be an equalizer in adding a little weight to her side of the "Teeter totter" or seesaw of attractiveness. So, in describing personality types, this "Barging tool" can many times even up the score and make up for deficiencies in several areas, and personality is only one of those areas.

MEN

Alright, we know what the women have in the equation of "Yin and yang", and how it seems to give balance to the whole balancing act, but how about the men. What do the men have to bring to this table of love...or lust.

Once again it depends on what women are looking for in a man, so let's just explore some of those things. For most women beyond the looks category, they are going to focus on security. This is also dependent on their lifestyle and what they are use to. Do they have children that need to be provided for, taken care of, and brought up in a manner that they respect. If so, this man must project a level of potential security, such as a stable job, profession or business owner. This whole picture of security can swing the scales of him being just ok, to "Let's do this" for the woman, even if the man is not on the cover of Guess Magazine, or even "Mad Magazine". Men are the providers, and the protectors of the women & the family. They will always be looked upon in this manner as they have been for thousands of years, and the more stable you look, the more weight you'll have on the seesaw of love, no matter what you look like.

Oh 'ya, and though a man's "Equipment" can be easily duplicated by any cucumber or hotdog, there's nothing like the "Real thing" which can also "Swing" things in the Man's favor and add "Weight" to the equation of attractiveness.

PEOPLE TYPES

MR. BOLD/MS. BEAUTIFUL

This person never has to work at getting someone by his/her side to share the evening, lunch, dinner, or a weekend in Vegas with them. They know (or think they do) what they want in a mate, or companion and they usually get it. Trouble is, they spend almost as many lonely nights as if they were the person on the bottom of the social totem pole, because no one they meet is ever good enough for them. When they do meet someone who they think IS "Good enough for them", that person is looking for someone "Better" than they are. So Mr. Bold or Ms. Beautiful, has to "Settle" for the 2nd best person in the bar, who intern thinks they (Mr.Bold/Ms.Beaut) are just "What the doctor ordered". Now you have what is considered a "Weighted" relationship, which means one of them thinks, "I'm better than you and you know it, so you'll have to work harder at pleasing me". Sometimes that person thinks, "OK, I'll work at it, I'll string him/her along, they're "Arm candy", sure "Let's do this!" Finally they get tired of "Doing this", and its "See 'ya, I'm back in action again". Another waste of time for both of them. They got together because of the wrong VALUES. It always ends up to be values, and what kind of values each person has adopted. When they don't align it's break up time, but it just may take longer.

Mr./Ms CONTROLLER

This person likes to always be in control, take control, direct the action, and be the beneficiary of the end result. They don't like it when challenged, or don't have an answer to every question they are asked. A tell tale sign could be that they answer every question WITH a question, and they're hard to get a straight answer from. They are usually one step ahead of the action taking place, and are very quick to notice everything around them, especially out of the corner of their eye. They usually have a jealous streak and are always on the lookout for the man/woman who would take you away from them, because they are very weak in their self-image or self-esteem. This may come from past experiences of cheating spouses, bad business deals where they were cheated, ugly divorces, and an entire host of experiences where they came out #2. As good test to see if they fit into this controller category is to keep track of how man times they surrender their plans to yours, or let you make the decision. If it's less than 50/50 you've got a controller type, and YOU'VE got to make a decision.

MR./MS NEEDY

This person is the exact opposite of the controller type. They NEED someone to tell them what to do, where to eat, what to have for lunch, dinner, and more. They would be a perfect match for the controller, but then again controllers don't like the needy because they're too easy to control, and they need a challenge. A good ear mark for the needy person, is that they are always bombarding you with endless questions. This is sometimes better than the "Blabber", who never shuts up, because you get a chance to voice your feelings or opinions. However, they still want to put most of the responsibility on you for planning everything, from where or what you'll do for dinner, recreational activity, what you think of their friends, which doctor would be best, which school is best for the kids if they have any, and on and on. It can drive you crazy after a while.

MR./MS DRAMA

For this person getting out of bed is a crisis, let alone making a decision where to have lunch. They thrive on adversity, and turmoil in their life, and want to bring it into yours. They are not satisfied when things are operating on an even keel, or harmonious manner. They NEED to have some kind of a problem so they can solve it, make it right, or put down that "Inconsiderate" person that caused it all. When you first meet up with them it isn't but a few minutes that they begin to tell you a "Story" of how they were taken advantage of, mistreated, or have to even the score with another person. This person is easy to spot because of this type of behavior that stands out like a flashing red neon sign saying, "I'm trouble!" Maybe you're the kind of person who needs this kind of trouble, but once again, the outside packaging can make up for the inside time bomb, and some people think, "He's so good looking, how bad can it be, let's give it a shot." Or, "She's enough to drive you out'a your mind, but what a body, use me 'till 'ya use me up." Once again. this is a perfect example of a symbiotic relationship.

This person also has a great need to be TOLD how wonderful they are, and on a regular basis. If not, they think there's something wrong, their self-worth has not been validated in the last hour. They start to feel depressed until you, the vision of positive energy, lift them up again.

Remember, for everyone, there's someone to match them. If that's what you want, go for it.

MR./MS. TALKER

Did you ever meet someone who seems like they had too many espressos, taken the wrong upper drug, or puts the A in "A type" personality? They just can't seem to shut up, except to take a breath, and you are thinking "Why doesn't someone call me on my cell phone?" Or, "Can I get arrested for THINKING about killing someone?" So you find some way to break into the one-way conversation to say you've got to go the bathroom etc.

This is a perfect example of someone who is trying their best to impress you by giving you as much information about themselves as they can in the shortest amount of time. This because they've seen you looking at your watch, and they recognize that "Long tail cat in a room full of rocking chairs", look on your face, and they know you're going to be bolting very soon.

HOLD ON, this may be a diamond in the rough, a blessing in disguise. This behavior CAN be corrected, once the person begins to realize you are interested, and they don't have to try, try, try any more to impress you. In this case you may want to just jump in there and try to slow things down, do a lot of smiling, and speak in a very controlled, as well as slower rate and tone. Depending upon what other attributes this person may have, it just may be in your best interests to look further into this personality type. The fact that they re trying to win you over, impress you and make you attracted to them, may be in your favor, if you like what you see. Some personality traits are deal breakers, and some can be altered when the person knows there is a NEED for this alteration. They might even not know they are doing it, whatever IT is. If they're values are along your same lines, then all YOU have to do is let them know that they need to "Bring it down" a little bit, just relax a little more, which will give you a chance to get to know them better if there is a two way communication between you both.

But, there is a chance that someone a long time before you came along, has tried the very same thing, to no avail and given up as you may well do. It just depends on the person, how much effort do you want to go to, and what you think the benefits will be if there are any. But when you step back and look at it, doesn't that describe any undertaking in life involving WORK. JUST DO IT!

THE PERFECTIONIST

This person will probably NEVER find their "One and only" because they don't exist. They have this value system in their head that says, "There's always something wrong with everyone". The trouble with this person is that they themselves are not perfect, and they project their own faults in someone else if it is at all possible.

So let's explore what IS perfect. What are they looking for? Someone said to be a good wife you need to be chief in the kitchen, a whore in the bedroom, a German engineer in the garage, and a psychotherapist all the time.

If you're a man you need to be a Playgirl model, a great cook, a French lover in the bedroom, and a great listener all the time.

The perfectionist is always looking for that negative part of a person's personality, they are always trying to uncover that chink in someone's "Armor", and just can't wait until they find it to say, "See I told 'ya so, they're not perfect." This person has a negative based reality, and if they could clone themselves they would STILL be unhappy with the results, because their counterpart would be too much like them, and THAT would be the problem presenting itself.

You can refer to the old bar room toast, "Here's to the girl I'm looking for, she's deaf and dumb and owns a liquor store."

Finding just the right person for YOUR personality, lifestyle, and level of energy may mean finding someone that is NOT like you at all, with all their imperfections, negativities, and faults.

If you use the criteria of how much HARMONY you both have when you're together, you will begin to lose that "He/She's got to be perfect" syndrome, and begin to see many more people with "Possibilities" that you may have passed on when you had the chance to become good friends first of all, and then took the relationship to another higher level. So, drop the perfectionist attitude and realize that it's how well each of you can "Fit" the other person without a tremendous amount of work, and bending over backwards to accommodate them, their life style personality, and just being with them. Realize it's YOU that just may have to change to find someone that fills your empty space, and brings love into your life. JUST DO IT.

CHAPTER 27

DATING IN THE MODERN WORLD

You remember when you had to call (or received a call) from someone to ask them out, or be asked out on a date? You couldn't leave them a message on a "Machine", you couldn't "Text" them a "Let's get together" message, or email them a note? You should have felt lucky. A while back before there were even any phones, a boy had to knock on a girl's door or see her in person to ask her out, and it was to take her to a function where there was always a lot of people, they were almost never alone.

A lot has changed since then and one of the most important things that has changed with years, has been a thing called VALUES. With that in mind, let's focus on the values people now possess, and how it relates to new technological advances of the modern age. These advances have given an entirely new face to the dating scene, how people meet, become friends, and take their relationship to a higher level.

It use to be if you wanted to ask a girl out, you

had to knock on her (or her parents) door, meet the family and then go to a social event WITH the family where there were always a lot of people, and you were very rarely never alone together. This behavior was brought about by VALUES. Some of these values were religion based, some were just common sense, but most of the values by which people evaluated someone are much the same today. Once you get out of high school, finish college (if you're fortunate enough to go there anyway), and take your place as a wage earner in society, you should have begun to acquire a certain set of these VALUES.

Sometimes the word values, can be seen as ultimate truths carved in stone...we THINK. Then as we go through a few more years of life we change some of these "Truths" as we know them, and begin to believe they were carved in "Styrofoam" instead of concrete, and begin to change some of these hard and fast beliefs which are now labeled as VALUES.

Ex: One of your beliefs taught to you by your parents: "Every time you tell a lie, something bad happens." You grow up being more truthful than not, then once you tell a lie and nothing bad happens. You begin to re-evaluate that statement, and tell another lie...nothing goes wrong, the Earth is still on it's axis, and life goes on. Now your belief system is forming another set of these VALUES caused by your personal history. Which by the way is the main reason we REALLY believe the way we do, even if we SAY we believe differently. But back to values, people tend to attract, and BE attracted to people who have the same values as themselves. Once again, you attract what you are, but in this case as it relates to the dating scene (or when in the "Looking for someone" mode) the values you have adopted for yourself can either attract or repel the "Right" people, or the "Wrong" people. This has been one of the truths, and still holds true, if you were in the 1800s or yesterday at Joe's Bar and Grille.

So how has today's dating scene changed so radically from what it use to be 25 years ago. Let's examine a few of the main areas.

COMMUNICATION

Communication has got to be the highest

element of interaction, because we communicate on so many more levels than just our speech, and with so many different medias of delivery and reception. Let's take for example the main media of communication we can all recognize as probably most important, the telephone.

Now it's not JUST the telephone, you have the cell, or mobile phone which places a multitude of communication choices at your fingertips. Let's examine how these choices help us or hurt us.

Several of these glittering pieces of gold could be real gold or a "Bear trap" of technology.

CELL PHONES

EASE OF CONTACT - Good or BAD? - It's nice to be able to reach someone instantly, and hear their voice, how did they like our date last night, can we see each other again, how about lunch? GOOD THING.

They call you and want to do "Face time"... you're with someone else at lunch or dinner, BAD THING. You are not looking so good, you don't feel too good, or just don't want to talk, but because they hear your phone ringing they know it is on, and wonder why you're not answering, BAD THING. This all comes down to communication NOT WANTED! Someone who THINKS you like them, want to see them, and can't wait to talk to them is ringing your phone off the hook, but you don't answer. BAD THING!

TEXTING - People have now gotten in the texting "Frenzy" of communication, and it has totally changed the level and TYPE of interaction we now either enjoy, or hate. You cannot attach an intimacy level to the text, you cannot convey the same level of FEELING you would if you were actually talking to them. If you miss-type one letter of word it can give an entirely different meaning to the sentence. BAD THING

Some people have said that they would rather text than *talk* to someone BECAUSE of the fact it takes **away** intimacy. They don't WANT the other person to hear their voice and the deep down meaning it may convey.

PHOTOS from phones - Now you can send photos to each other - GOOD.

THE INTERNET - GOOD & BAD

You have a wide variety of people to choose from with a wide scope of interests, likes and dislikes. Many more people to interact with - GOOD THING

Other people have a wide variety of people besides you to choose from, your competition is stiffer - BAD THING

DATING SITES ARE MORE PLENTYFULL Because of the cost, this separates the more affluent from the less professional and financially secure people. If you're one of the former this is good for you, in that it eliminates people that are not either UP TO or equal to your academic standard.

Remember this: Academic accomplishment should not be your only criterion for assigning a yes or no to someone's desirability, only a guide line. There are plenty of "Perfect match" people out there with no PhD, no Masters degree and no BA in whatever, and they could be your total answer to who you're looking for. So go back to the "Harmony quotient" of life. Natural harmony is something that can't be "pre-ordained" or have a flashing sign above someone's head saying "This is it!" or "Take this one!"

The dating sites have made things easier to access more partners, but in so doing have given you so many more choices, and intern made your job many times more difficult because of these multitude of choices. Now there are many more "Frogs" and "Frogettes" to kiss. So...maybe a handshake would be better to start of with, and safer.

SPEED DATING

This is a new type of social interaction usually put on by a large dating site or organization. You have 5 minutes to be with another person of the opposite sex and learn something about them, while telling them something about you, that is suppose to be attractive to them. It could be fun, just for the one time experience, or a waste of your time and money. It comes under the heading of if you haven't tried it don't knock it. Who knows, if you're thinking, "Nobody I would ever be interested in, would do this", maybe there IS someone else in the room who is thinking the same thing, and BINGO...a match made in Heaven.

If nothing else if gives you practice in meeting new people you may never see again, so don't worry or care what they think of you, and let it all hang out...be yourself. That's what they want to see any way so JUST DO IT!

DATING SITES

Computers have added so much to our lives and at the same time complicated them by becoming so indispensible. Dating sites on the web have sprung up like weeds in a Texas barn lot, and each one tries to convince you that you're going to meet just the perfect person for you and you alone. They have you fill out an exhaustive personal information data sheet that looks more like an IRS audit, so you can meet the same person you met the night before in the local pub.

GO FISHING

When you think about it, finding just the right person for you and you alone, is a lot like fishing, and there's a lot of fish in the sea.

If you go fishing and you throw out one line, that's one hook on one rod, you have one hook in the water, what are your chances of catching something? If you throw out 4 rods with 1 hook each, now you have 4 chances of catching a fish. But, if you throw out 4 rods that have a quadruple hook rig (4 hooks per rod) now you have 16 chances of catching something you can take home for dinner! The same thing goes for you, when finding someone, "To take home for dinner!"

In the beginning it's just a numbers game, and the *amount* of single people you meet increases the chances that one of them will turn out to be the one that you're looking for, with just the right characteristics.

But, don't forget this:

THE LAW OF DIMINISIONING RETURNS

An increase in a productive factor applied

beyond a certain point fails to bring about a proportional increase in the end result.

In other words, once you get past meeting a certain amount of single people it doesn't seem like meeting more people is the answer.

In this case, meeting CERTIAN kinds of people will make the difference. This is called "Efficiency", and it's also been termed as "Working smart" instead of working hard. The question here is, what can you do to work smart?

THE SHOTGUN APPROACH OR YOUR FIRST IMPRESSION?

There are two schools of thought here. One is to meet as many people as possible, say "Hi" to every person that you're attracted to (not wearing a wedding ring) with in 20 ft. of your location. This is known as the "Working hard" approach, and does have some merit, but "Burnout" is a distinct possibility and then you get the reputation of the "Wolf who has never had a meal", and pretty soon no one will talk to you, even the other "Wolves".

But, if you take the attitude of "Nothing ventured nothing gained" you have to get some degree of positive results sooner or later.

FIRST IMPRESSION: What is your first thought about someone the instant you meet them, or more important, have a CHANCE to meet them. Do they give you a glance, or smile, do THEY start a conversation with you? If that's the case then you would be wise in spending a little extra effort on getting to know this person, some of their background, what they like and don't like etc. All that of course would depend upon how attracted you are to this person, and your instant first impression of them. Pretty soon you will get better and better at evaluating your "Perfect match" with is he/she the right height, weight, hair color, body type, age etc.

SPECALIZED GROUPS

These are clubs, organizations or groups that have one central theme, athletic, intellectual, dancing, physical (tall club), or something that is focused on one specific area of interest. This way you are more assured of meeting people with like interests. This is been proven more effective that the "Shotgun" approach to meeting new people.

What do you like to do? Is it sports, knitting, sky diving, scuba diving, skiing, or whatever, just ask yourself that question. What would you do all day long, every day until you got sick and tired of it? Then search the Internet for that kind of activity group. There is a very interesting web site called www.meetup.com and it is a site that has just about every type of group you can think of, that puts on events related to that kind of activity. For example: *Catholic Singles, that like fly fishing and blond tabby cats."*(just kidding, but you get the idea)

Now you have to believe that's a pretty selective group of people, but I'll bet everybody there likes "Everybody there". Why is that? They've got SOMETHING IN COMMON!

This is not rocket science!

When I was in school getting my 2nd degree in education I took a beginning class in Psychology. According to an exhaustive study by some psychotherapist guru, they came up with this "Holy grail" of findings after interviews with hundreds of people in the form of a truth that should be written across the sky in 100 foot letters..."YOU WILL LIKE PEOPLE THAT LIKE YOU, and you will not people who DON'T like you!

I'm thinking, "This is what I paid my immense amount of tuition to find out? I needed to go to college to learn THIS? I wanted to either ask for my money back, or apply for a job as professor of psychology, maybe head of the department.

What's the bottom line here? As humans going from day to day, interfacing with many different types of culture, and personalities we tend to gravitate to people like us. We ATTRACT people TO us that are LIKE us. Once again, you attract what ARE.

When (and if) you are happy, you attract people who are happy. When you are positive, and have positive mannerisms, you attract people that are positive and have the same mannerisms. Dating in today's society is more complicated, there are many more people in the general population, and with the Internet you have many more choices.

It's up to you to USE those choices, and variables to your advantages to provide more and more people to interact with and therefore be more selective in making that big decision when you've found someone that seems to have the winning qualifications and just right parameters you're looking for.

If you're not computer savvy, LEARN a little bit about computers, you can buy a cheap laptop for under $100. Get a friend to show you how to access the web and put yourself out there on one of the dating sites, and get a social media page like Twitter or Facebook. Then Mr./Ms. potential "Just right for you" will be calling YOU!

CHAPTER 28

REPELLING THE WRONG PERSON

(FOR WOMEN)

This is somewhat of a chapter repeat, but slanted toward the feminine side of the equation.

Since women are more on the receiving end of the man/women pursuit situation, this section is slanted in their direction more than for men.

Sooner or later you must have heard someone say the following, "I just seem to attract all the wrong type of men."

It doesn't matter if you're super gorgeous, or if you're plane Jane, you are going to meet loads of people who want to take advantage of you, are not right for you, or in some cases not right for ANYONE!

Your success in finding that right person is largely depends on how quickly you can recognize this type of *wrong* person.

A friend of mine had a good analogy, he said, "When you first meet someone you think you could be interested in, look for marks all over their body from people touching then with 10 foot poles."

MEANING: If you get the slightest feeling that this person could be trouble, you're probably not the first person to have this perception, so keep it in the back of your mind for reference.

But back to the title of this chapter...the "Repelling" part. In this instance we are talking mostly to the women readers, since men don't usually have problems with *women* pursuing *them*, not taking "No" for an answer, and need a restraining order on them.

With women it's considerably different, in that the man is 95% of the time the pursuer, and if he didn't adopt the saying "When a woman says no, she means yes", as a mantra, our species would have never gotten off the ground.

But that time has long since come and gone, and women are many times faced with not only saying NO, but meaning HELL NO, and still it doesn't phase the male of the human species any more than the male of the ANY species. They just think if they don't get at least 3 rejections they're not doing their job selling themselves. In fact since I did write the book on sales (Winning at sales, it's a lot more money - Amazon.com) I can see how there are a lot of parallels in successful selling & closing deals, as related to meeting, impressing, and cultivating a relationship with members of the opposite sex. All you are doing is selling yourself, and since the "Product" is standing right there in front of the buyer, it's fairly easy to evaluate, at least on a physical level, THEN move to a mental level.

Since first impressions are usually made upon looks, you have a pretty good idea of your degree of like or dislike in another person when you first lay eyes on them, before they say anything. This is when the attracting or repelling first takes place. If you don't like what you see, don't be locking eyes with this person, or even "Accidently" catch their gaze, as they will invariably take it as a "Come hither" look, and suddenly, there they are! It doesn't matter if it's in a grocery store, lumber yard or nightclub the rules are always the same. Don't ACT interested if you're not.

It kind of comes under the heading of: "If you don't want a stray dog hanging around your place, DON'T FEED HIM, he'll go away...maybe."

As mentioned before if you know what you like, then you know what you DON'T like, and to repel somebody you have to keep from attracting them in the first place.

However, it greatly depends upon the type of person you are. If you are attractive, men are lining up to meet you, and the only worries you have are about their background, track record with women, (or police record), do you have Mace handy, and how will your personalities fit...if at all.

If you're *not* so bless with good looks then you may be of the school of "Anyone who talks to me can get to first base", type of attitude. Once again, let them in the front yard, next thing they're in the kitchen eating out of your dog bowl.

Phase II of Repelling

After the initial hello's and introductions are

over, and you decide he's not for you it's time to put plan B into execution. Which is to demonstrate using body language that says, *NOT INTERESTED.*

Some of this is looking at your watch, looking away while he's talking to you, acting like you didn't hear what he said, and finally having to "Go to the bathroom" if there is one. The physical environment you are in has a lot to do with separating you from him. If it's a public place like a grocery store (men think it's a great place to meet women) then you're on a mission and have got to finish shopping, so excuse yourself and do it.

Some men *can* take a hint, and it doesn't take much to make them think, "If she's not interested, then neither am I." When this type of guy gets a whiff of your disinterest, he's gone. Which means he's probably got a lot going for him, and he doesn't need you any more than you need him. Which, by the way is a good level of balance for both people.

Neither one NEEDS the other, but it would be nice to be together and maybe CREATE a need.

But, we'll talk about that later. THIS is the guy you may want to hang on to, but for now let's explore the one for whom you carry your pepper spray (and you should).

This is the cave man type, who also is not too successful with women because he is always projecting this "Sexually hungry *Troglodyte attitude with the "Got to find a woman"...look. He's not giving up with just a subtle "Excuse me, I've got to go", line from you. This guy feels you are just playing hard to get and that turns him on even more so his efforts become more intense and he won't leave you alone. For this person you have to just come out and say these words, **"Leave me alone, I'm not interested in you, could NEVER be interested in you and if you want I can have someone else here explain that to you!**

If that doesn't do it you have a problem and I am not going to make any (but I could) recommendations, except to learn self-defense.

And I am VERY serious about that! DO IT!

*Prehistoric Cave dweller

CHAPTER 29

HOW HAPPY ARE YOU?

Since you attract what you are, and you want to attract someone who IS happy...how happy you are determines how "Happy" a person you will attract.

STOP READING NOW and answer this question:

WHAT WAS THE HAPPIEST DAY OF YOUR LIFE?

Write the answer below:

Use the criterion of how it has changed your life for the better, the amount of joy it gave you and your life in general, and are the people connected with it still a part of your life?

Most people have never asked themselves this question and therefore it really causes you to evaluate your life's history, where you've been, what you think is important, and where you're going, or even *IF* you know where you're going.

This is not a deep question that requires or should require a lot of thought. If you have to spend a lot of time trying to decide, you REALLY need to take stock of your life, what you think you want from life and from yourself.

You have a choice every day when you wake up, you can be happy or you can be something other than happy. The trouble is this, it takes WORK to be happy, and most people need to be reminded to BE happy. They go from place to place, home to work, to lunch, back to work, then back to home without so much as a single thought about how great lunch was, how wonderful their life is in it's present state, how they have a roof over their heads, and a whole lot of other things that other people DON'T have.

They never think, "Gee I'm so happy I don't have Cancer!" So, why does it take a brush with Cancer, (with themselves or a loved one) to make someone thankful that they don't have it? Why can't you just develop a more positive personality, and a more positive way of looking at things, without having to experience, the problem first?

It's because of the way we were raised. Most children (according to several studies) have received 600,000 bits of negative information, statements, and negative influences before they are 10 years old.

That's because that's the way their parents were raised, and so on and so on.

HISTORY AXIOM:

HISTORY REPEATS ITSELF, BECAUSE IT REPEATS ITSELF

How about that for a "Head banger" of an illustration. Our minds and our mannerisms are like a tape recording, that re-records over and over in a loop until someone says, "Hey wait a minute here, I'm tired of stepping in the same bear trap every time I put my foot here, so I'll just walk home a different way".

In this manner the "Loop" gets changed, and the same thing is prevented from happening in the same way, producing the same results, getting the same reaction from the same people, just on a different day.

Now people don't have to say, "Gee why didn't I see THAT coming a mile off." The trouble with a lot of people is, that they need to step in the bear trap "Umpteen" times to remember to take a different path around it. People tend to be creatures of habit, even if those habits are bringing them results that they view as unsatisfactory, unwanted, and don't like. They seem to think that some how, some way, it's going to be "Different" this time, and things are going to turn out all fuzzy and wonderful just because it's a different day, different person, or situation. **WRONG!**

I'm sure you don't need to read the definition of insanity, but in case you're too young to know it, or have been fired by a boss for making the same mistakes over and over again, and he/she told you to look it up, and you haven't... here it is:

INSANITY: Doing the same thing, the same way over and over again expecting different results each time.

Doing things the same way for no good reason just because someone *tells* you to do it that way, comes under the same umbrella of insanity.

Each time you experience LEARNING it is because you EMPLOY something new that you have picked up, and found that it *does* change the outcome of the end result. Maybe not totally good or bad, but the results ARE different. Now you're closer to making your own choices without outside help, which may...again...be better, or not.

If you have received instructional information or a "Tip" on how to improve your situation, whatever that situation is (in this case we're talking about relationships) and you employ that instruction without questioning it even a little bit, evaluating the person it came from, or testing it out in a small or "Beta" format, you're like the guy/girl who jumps off the 30 ft. high diving board without first checking to see if there's any water in the pool, just because they figured there SHOULD be water in there.

Many people will give you advice, say you should be "This way" or do it, "This way" and you look at them and think, "You've been divorced 3 times 6 kids, on welfare, and you're going to give me advice on relationships? NOT!

Here's a little example of why things are done in a certain way.

STORY:

"We've Always Done it That Way"

Once upon a time, at a holiday dinner there was this large family gathering at the parent's home. All the children, brothers and sisters, aunts and uncles etc., were there to have a wonderful dinner. One of the daughters was newly married and naturally was with her new husband. He noticed that when his wife was helping prepare the large piece of meat to be roasted she took a knife and cut about 2 inches off of the end, then put it in the roasting pan with the potatoes, and vegies etc. He immediately asked, "Honey, why did you cut off the end of the roast?" She replied, "Well, that's the way Mom has always done it, that's the way it's done." He then asked, "WHY?" She said, "Just because...and quit asking stupid questions." He went to her Mother (his new Mother-in-Law) and asked her why SHE always cut the end off the piece of meat. She said, "Well...that's the way my Mother always did it, that's the way it's always been done, that's what we do, what a stupid question." So he went to the Great Grandmother and asked her, "Why did you always cut the end of the big roast off before putting it in the pan?" She replied, "Well, grandpa was a butcher, and he would bring the best and biggest piece of meat home for the big dinner and if I didn't cut the end off, it wouldn't fit in the pan. What a stupid question, why do you ask?"

What's this got to do with meeting (or attracting) that special "Right" person?

If you're not attracting the kind of potential partner that you want to attract, you need ask yourself, "What am I doing that isn't working"? You need to prevent history from "Repeating itself" and step in, make some changes, take stock of what you're doing. If you've *always done something* a certain way, and you don't like the results, do it a DIFFERENT way and see what happens. You might not like the new result, but at least it won't be the SAME result you've been getting.

Sometimes it's best just to do things different just for the sake of doing things different. It will also help you get use to that thing we all hate, called CHANGE.

People don't like change, and will continue to "Sit on a prickly Cactus of life" complaining about how much it hurts, because (according to them) it's too much trouble, or they're just too tired to move.

Finding the right partner is one thing, and it means you have to do a lot of LOOKING for this person, and it's a lot of WORK.

It's much more work than *ALLOWING* the right person to come into your life. This word *allowing* should be examined more closely, because it's just as important as the looking part.

ALLOWING: When you allow something to happen in your life, you don't "Get in the way" of it happening, by TRYING so hard to MAKE it happen, you step back and after visualizing it, expecting it, and planning for it to happen, then you quit trying, and ALLOW it to happen.

In the book "The Law of Attraction", by Jerry Hicks it talks about how we attract things, events, and people into our lives by the thoughts we are thinking. It says very simply, "You get what you think about most." So if you are wanting someone to share your life with, or just dinner, and you focus your thoughts on it with high emotion, and intent, then just relax and let it, or ALLOW it to happen, it becomes reality. It depends on how much emotion you attach to it, or how much you really, I mean really, want it. When it does come your way you then are thankful, and ACCEPT it realizing that this is the result of your power of thought, and accept the joy it brings in to your life.

Most people have this automatic response to something good or great happening in their life, that sounds like, "Wow, I can't *believe* this actually happened to ME." Or, "Are you kidding, I really won xxx, I don't believe it." The first thing they say is, "I don't believe it!"

However, when you are using the Laws of Attraction, you are EXPECTING this wonderful positive event, and nothing surprises you. Each time you "Materialize" your desires you become more powerful at doing it again, and drawing that special person to you, who is going to add joy and love to your life. This is just another phase of this power of attraction that we are given to use to enrich our lives.

There is a great line in the book Psych-Cybernetics that says:

"You are not happy because your world is right, your world is right because you are happy."

Think about that in depth, or in a slightly different way. Is it because things are going good for you that makes you happy, or is it because you ARE happy that causes things to be going good for you?

At some point if things are NOT going your way you have to break the cycle and BECOME happy even though you're far from that state of being.

Once again you attract what you are, so no matter what situation you happen to be in, there is a good chance it could be worse, so be thankful that your situations (whatever they are) have not evolved into that negative state. Just that level of positive realization is enough some times to turn things around, and get you on a positive note. Then good things begin to happen again. **SMILE a lot,**(even if you don't feel like it) it puts you into a much more positive state automatically.

Suddenly because you are now on a more positive note, this ALLOWS you to meet someone who sparks a new level of energy, and a new outlook in you and your perception of life in general. You begin to feel more confident, and pretty soon feel like you can accomplish anything.

Your job seems to get easier, people seem to be more friendly, the day seems to look brighter, more positive, and it just gets better and better as the days go by. Probably not a lot has changed in all of the situations mentioned, except your PERCEPTION of the events mentioned.

Your job is still the same degree of difficulty, and responsibility, the people around you still treat you like they always have. It may be raining outside but you like the feeling of the cool raindrops on your face, and think to yourself, "What a great day this is."

Nothing has changed except YOU! With your positive level of energy, even in the face of adversity, you and only you, turned things around, YOU drew to you that special person that may have walked right by or even turned away from you sensing your negative attitude or energy, because things were not working out for you at the moment.

That is the definition of a winner, someone who can take a negative situation and turn it into a positive one, and people like to be around a winner.

You attract what you are, like attracts like and how you draw someone to you is by showing the Universe that you have the power to project good, in the face of negativity.

You're thinking "That's easy for you to say, you haven't been faced with xxx or had to xxx, and *your* (the reader's) personal situation is entirely different from anything this writer has experienced.

We all have challenges, and walls we think are insurmountable, but all we have to do is make it over ONE of those walls, and we realize we have the power to do it again, over a bigger wall and then even a bigger one.

With this idea we have changed our belief system, and this belief system tells us that no matter WHO you are, you would be lucky to have us as a dinner date, or to say "I Do", for the rest of our lives, IF that's what we wanted.

With that kind of confidence going for you who would not be attracted to you? Which brings us back to that earlier chapter about how self-confidence is one of the greatest attractants you possess.

Let's not confuse self-confidence with arrogance, or ego or any other of the "Personal repellants" you can think of that would make you seem like you're in love with yourself, or you think you're the next thing to "The most interesting man in the world."

But back to your level of happiness and how it affects your life. When you are in a happy or positive state of mind, you not only draw that special person you've been looking for to you like a magnet, but also draw a multitude of good things your way as a by-product of that happiness.

As mentioned before, you have a choice when you wake up each morning, to be happy or be something else other than happy.

Most people actually forget that fact. It's easy to FORGET to BE happy unless you have a note on your bathroom mirror that says, "Be happy". So, do that, put a note somewhere you will see easily, that just says…HAPPY.

When things are going in a "Just ok" manner it's like Luke warm water. You don't feel it against your skin, like you would if it were colder or hotter than normal. So a lot of people spend most of their time in a state of "Limbo" between being happy and "NOT sad".

They never go outside and say, "Wow what a beautiful day, it's not too sunny and not too cloudy, not too hot and not too cold, it's WONDERFUL!

To be able to capture this "Everyday" positive realization of how great things actually are, you need to remember to DO IT! Just the act of realizing these wonderful and positive things around you puts you into an also wonderful positive STATE. This is the state that gives your thoughts energy and power.

Now, back to the Laws of Attraction...YOU ATTRACT WHAT YOU ARE!

If you are in this positive state of joy and awareness you're thinking of positive things and if one of them is meeting someone who is just right for you...all you have to do is ALLOW it to happen.

And it WILL happen!   **JUST DO IT!**

CHAPTER 30

PUTTING IT ALL TOGETHER

So how many of you are reading this last chapter first?

GOTCHA !

A lot of people tend to do this because they want instant gratification, instant ROI, and their whole existence from the time they make their first dollar is, "Boil it down for me...what's the bottom line, when do we go to lunch, when's quitting time, and when to I get paid?

If this is you, you've wasted your money on this book, because you won't believe, let alone employ anything you've read...IF you choose to read it, because you think you know it all and there's nothing that can help you or your "Situation" whatever that situation is.

If you're reading this as the last chapter after going through and CONTEMPLATING the other chapters, there IS hope for you, and you do have it within your grasp to make the necessary changes to affect your entire life, attract that special person you've been looking for and start experiencing the first level of...JOY!

So what to we mean by the phrase putting it all together? First of all we have to assume that we *don't* have it "All together" initially, or we wouldn't be reading a book about putting it all together...to attract just the right person for US into our lives.

EXPERIENCE

Most of us are a product of relationship experience, meaning the only guidance we've received about relationships is what we've learned first hand, or by experience, (good judgment comes from experience, and a lot of that comes from bad judgment), and lastly by observing our parents, and or friends.

After all who ever *listens* to their PARNETS about relationships especially when they might not have been the most harmonious examples of the male/female interaction to observe when growing up in the home life?

From there we move on to observing our friends and their relationships...another bad idea.

Your friends will give you advice as if it was written by Dr. Ruth herself, because they've had tons of "experience", most of that on the negative side. The tell tale signs of this usually start with the phrases like, "Don't ever date a guy/girl that ____, and you fill in the blank, because that's what happened to them, it was a disaster, and the same thing is suppose to happen to you. WRONG!

Each person and situation is different, and how you handle it is different, so consider the source of your "Advice" when you here the words, "Don't ever xxxx xxx. Nothing is cut and dried, or black & white, and a lot of what you learn is, as they say, "On the job" training. The trouble with OJT as it relates to real life, is that sometimes you're faced with "Trainers" who have no "Training". These people don't know any more than you do as to what is going on, but try to tell you what to do, how to act, and what course of action you should take.

Wouldn't it be nice if we could have a crystal ball and actually look into the future to see how things are going to "Play out?" That's what this book is suppose to help you do. None of us has a crystal ball, but we do have a thing called INTUITION, and this intuition helps us make choices that either alter the future or repeat the past, IN the future.

It all goes back to the definition of the word "Learning" as I've mentioned before. If you don't APPLY the new information you acquire and the same negative pendulum hanging over your head comes down and cuts you in half...again, then you haven't LEARNED anything!

The good or best level of judgment you use in most situations has to have come from experience, and at least half of *that* experience has been associated with BAD JUDGEMENT. Unless of course you've been really lucky at picking winners, when you don't know what a winner is to begin with or...you are reading this book before you've had one serious relationship. THEN you've got a road map to go by, and a set of parameters to help you make some choices, or educated guesses.

If you're reading this book and saying at the same time, "Yah I did that, Oh yah, that was me too", then hopefully it has strengthened your resolve to make some changes, alter some belief systems, and attract some different results than you've been experiencing.

When we say "Putting it all together" first of all let's define what "IT" is.

IT - Is a collective of many different ideas, concepts, truths, from many different schools of thought, experts, experiences, about the interaction, relationships, attraction and repulsion of heterosexual human beings.

These human beings are greatly evolved from the prehistoric days when the male just took the female by force if he was big enough, strong enough, and had a big enough club. It was nature's way to insuring the survival of the species, by allowing the biggest, strongest, smartest male to spread his seed, giving the Homo Sapiens species a fighting chance to survive and evolve in a very harsh environment.

Thanks to that evolvement we are now faced with another problem of male "Finding" female, that's not a big problem. The big problem is male being HAPPY with female and vs/versa.

Wouldn't it be nice if you could just enter another person's mind and see everything that's there, all the fears, judgments, triumphs, victories, and losses. Then you could make a judgment on WAY many more things than just if you might be able to get along.

Maybe it's good we can't actually really and truly DO that, but as you've read about NLP, there are ways of getting into a person's mind, psyche, personality, and mental state that will tell you a lot about that person. Their level of credibility, honesty, truthfulness, and give you a better than average look at who they really are.

This book is the road map that helps you work on those "Mysteries without any clues", shows you where the light switch is located within that dark room called reality, and gets you asking yourself questions like, "What qualities do I really want in someone to share my life with?"

Once you find that light switch, then it's up to you to turn it on, and depending WHO'S switch you're flicking, (yours or someone else's) be ready for an awaking that may shock you.

But one way or another, once you SEE the problem, now you can FIX the problem. The big question is, do you WANT to fix it or do you like it broken the way it is?

Most people resist change so much that although something is causing them pain, they've had it for so long that they begin to LIKE the pain because they've gotten use to it, and hate to change even though they know it will IMPROVE their situation.

If this is you, ask yourself the question, "If I am in a valley, even a comfortable one, what would the view look like from the mountain top?" You'll never know until you climb up there, you may want to go there just to "Visit", then if you still like the valley (and some do) climb back down, but you won't keep wondering what it's like up there anymore.

As it relates to this book about finding or attracting just the perfect person for you (if there is one) there a couple of questions you should be asking yourself.

1. *How long should I keep on looking?* The answer to this question should be another question: How bad do you want to find that special someone? Here's a concept for you: "Enjoy the journey more than destination." Meaning, when you enjoy the search, the interaction, and all that goes with it, suddenly you become more effective in everything you do, not just the search for that special someone. Life begins to take on a new dimension for you. You see, or realize things you never realized before, or see a side of people that you never knew existed. If you begin to live like you've ALREADY found that perfect someone, it increases the power of your "Attraction magnet" tremendously, and things and people begin to come your way all by themselves. When you are exercising the power within you to just BE happy, joyous, and noticing all the good around you, that is when you begin to enjoy the journey more than wanting to even ARRIVE at the destination.

Everyone in our society is so "Destination oriented" and they not only forget how enjoyable the journey COULD be, that they even forget the "Directions" on how to get there, or try and write their own map. Some of them come up with a few "Short cuts" on that map that they think will get them to their destination faster, quicker, and more efficiently than the "Old" way. The trouble with "Cutting corners" is, that corner you just cut off to save time has the information on it that you were looking for containing the secret to getting what you were looking for in the first place!

Finding the right person, winning at love, or being a winner at anything, has several different phases, and each one has it's own timing. When you realize this and ALLOW things to happen at the speed and timing they were meant to happen, NOW you are in the "Pocket" of positive energy, and guess what...YOU'RE the one controlling that energy phase, not it controlling you.

This is a concept very few people have ever learned, and may never learn, because it is not determined by how HARD you work, how FAST you run, or how much FORCE you use, but how well you ALLOW it to happen, get out of the way and let your positive actions and imagery complete their mission.

Love is something you can only attract, you can't "Catch it", put it in a bottle, or a cage, take it out an play with it when you feel like it, you have to make it WANT to stay with you, by mirroring it and return to it what it gives to you, so that it can once again mirror you.

THE MIRROR EFFECT

Once I had an apartment that had mirrored glass doors on the closet that faced the large mirror over the sink in the bathroom. It produced a hundred, or more, reflections of reflections.

If you've ever been presented with this situation you know that each mirror reflects the image in front of it, and it goes back into infinity because there is no end to the amount of times light can be reflected back on to itself.

Love is just like that set of mirrors, when you give love to the "Right" person, it is reflected back to you at which time you reflect right back the same love. We'll call this the MIRROR EFFECT, and it works the same way in almost every situation in life, you get back what you project. So, if you're getting back garbage and negativity, and you are not happy with the way people are treating you, then you need to look at the way you're projecting yourself, and your attitude.

You are becoming a product of the "Mirror effect". You are getting back the same attitude, feelings, and acceptance OR rejection that you are putting out.

It doesn't matter if we are talking about trying to meet (or attract) that special person, conduct a business deal, or attract a new client for your business, it's all the same principal of attraction or repulsion.

YOU ATTRACT WHAT YOU ARE!

The only way to know what you are projecting into the Universe is by looking at what is coming *to* you. If you don't like what you're getting, take a closer look at what you're putting out.

SELF-QUESTIONARE

Ask yourself the following questions about how you are trying to find (or attract) that special person that you feel will compliment your existence. If you are honest with the answers you hear inside your head (and you can't escape hearing them because they are coming from you TO you) these pieces of information should give you a better insight and clearer picture of your quest to attract, or find and then recognize that person with which you are meant to be.

1. Have I found that person that I thought may have been right for me, and passed them by?

1a. If it did pass them by what was the reason that made me do it? _____

2. Should I put more work into ATTRACTING that "Perfect" person rather that LOOKING for them? _____

2a. What are the things I can do to improve my chances of meeting or attracting this person? Put a check mark in the box when you have completed the task.

Physical appearance:

- [ ] Lose ____ lbs.
- [ ] Grooming Improved by_____
- [ ] Clothing Chg'd by_____

Mental Focus

3. Do I really know what I want? If so what is it?

_____

_____

Before going to sleep have I counted all the good things that happened to me today? Use another piece of paper (if needed) to keep track of all the good things that happened to you...TODAY.

Monday

Tuesday

Wednesday

Thursday

Friday

Saturday

Sunday

CHAPTER 31

BONIS SECTION

MAKE YOUR OWN MENTAL REPROGRAMMING TAPE OR CD

This section is dedicated to giving you instruction on how to actually create your own reprogramming audio tape or CD. This can and will restructure your belief system and what you think you deserve, and can accomplish. All you have to do is LISTEN to it on a regular basis in a quiet controlled environment to experience the impactual results, and be the beneficiary of the changes it imparts on your belief systems and your life in general.

Here's the big question? How bad do you really want to make the changes to your own life, your own personality, and your own habits to attract or find this person that you feel will make a significant difference to your future happiness and therefore your future in general?

Most people think, "Oh well, if it happens it happens, and if it doesn't happen it's not meant to be, why knock yourself out?"

These are just the kind of people who are living a luke warm mediocre existence, hoping for the best, but planning for the worst, and taking whatever they get wondering why life is so difficult or unfair.

If you want to BE happy, you have to CREATE HAPPY, and make it so. The "Blind squirrel" found the nut in the snowstorm because...why?

*BECAUSE HE WAS **LOOKING** FOR IT!*

The winner of the Mega Lotto won it because why? *THEY BOUGHT A TICKET!*

Now it's time to buy your ticket a ticket to happiness, and more life fulfillment. Here are a few things you can do to make it so.

THE SUBCONSCIOUS MIND

Almost all of our outward behavior is controlled by our SUB-conscious mind, this tells us what we THINK we can achieve, what we THINK we deserve, and many times gives us a PRE-conceived foregone conclusion as to a potential out come of an event happening in real time or in the future.

Many times this pre-conceived notion is derived from only ONE occurrence or happening in our personal history. Then because we remembered the result of that set of circumstances, this thinking caused us to believe that the same thing was bound to happen again, and of course IT DID! Now we've got a behavioral pattern that is destined to be repeated, not because it's unchangeable, but because we BELIEVE we can't change it and therefore it keeps happening.

In sports we notice when one competitor gets beat by their opponent the first time they play, it seems like every time they engage this same opponent they lose to them, even though they have beaten other competitors of a higher ranking. They are remembering the past event thinking history will repeat itself. This type of situation is presented many times in our every day lives on many different occasions, and the original event that established the pattern of winning or losing was (or could have been) established years ago or even in childhood.

As previously stated:

PAST PERFORMANCE DOES NOT PREDICT FUTURE SUCCESS OR FAILURE IN END RESULTS OR ACHIEVEMENTS

The purpose of this book is to help show you how to attract or find that special person you've been looking for, to help you fill that spot in your life that you know needs filling. The trouble is, you may have to either get rid of certain habits you now have or acquire new habits you now lack, in order for this to happen.

So what is preventing you from making these changes when you've been trying for years to do so? Does it seem like the harder you try, the harder is becomes to change, and now you've finally given up?

In this section we are going to deal with the actual mechanics of making a tool that WILL change your behavioral patterns, and WILL give you new "Arrows" to put in your St. Valentine's Day quiver to help you present a more appealing package to someone of your potential affection.

We are not in any way going to try to change the outside packaging without first changing the inside package, because that inside package is what someone is really going to want, and what they will cling to when the going get's rough.

In the act or reprogramming the subconscious mind there are several rules you want to observe.

1. Change the INSIDE first and the outside changes as a by-product.

APPLICATION: BE happy and you'll attract happiness. BE positive and you'll attract positive people and opportunities.

2. The more you try to change on a conscious level the less success you will have.

APPLICATION: You can repeat a 100 times to yourself that you want to lose weight, but it's only going into the conscious mind, and has no effect on your behavior. But when you reprogram the SUBconscious with phrases like "I enjoy the feeling of being hungry, it tells me I'm losing weight, and getting stronger", then that's what your new belief system becomes and you eat less and WANT to eat less, and you DO lose weight.

When you reprogram your inner subconscious mind with "I enjoy the people I meet and attract more positive energy each day", and this becomes your new belief system, you suddenly start noticing the beauty around you and attract more and more beauty.

Those are just examples of the tip of the iceberg of mental reprogramming, but you can understand how changing your belief system will change your level of energy, and ability to attract someone of a similar views and level of positive energy.

Below is a mental reprogramming script that when read into a tape recorder or audio recording device, will create a relaxation reprogramming tool. When you listen to it on a regular basis it WILL change your belief system. and outlook on the world around you and in turn what you will attract and WHO you will attract from that moment on.

We are going to create a relaxation

reprogramming recording that will cause you to become in a very relaxed state both mentally and physically. This will in turn put you into a state of being highly suggestible, and open to subconscious reprogramming and or suggestions. This SUBconscious part of your inner mind is what gives you your belief systems. Once it is changed to be more positive it will remain that way causing your outward behavior to be the same level of positive awareness and attractiveness. It doesn't matter if you believe this or not, it's TRUE. Once your INNER mind believes it, it becomes YOUR truth, and then you begin to realize the outward changes. In other words suddenly...there's the person you've been looking for, and maybe if they've read this book...they're looking for YOU!

WHAT IS NEEDED

1. A simple hand held digital recorder or a recorder program for your computer. If you get a recorder program (a lot of new computers come with it) you can create a .WAV or mp3 audio file that can be played on any CD player, ipad or even an iPhone. You just put it on

record and talk into it.

2. An inexpensive headset. You don't have to pay hundreds of dollars (and you can easily) for a headset, but a good over the ear type will help isolate outside noises that can be distracting when trying to relax listening to the induction part of the script.

3. A VERY quiet place without distractions such as lawn mowers, construction noise, traffic sounds, people talking, and a host of other distracting noises.

4. TIME: You can't hurry up and relax, and one of the best benefits of this relaxation reprogramming effort is, you feel refreshed and re-energized when you come back to your normal state of awareness.

WHAT THIS IS

OK, let's call this what it really is, and that's Hypnotherapy, Hypnosis, being hypnotized, but nobody calls it that any more, because the media, the movies, and talk shows have given it a bad rap. They are trying to portray it as someone having control over you, making you do things you wouldn't normally, and a whole host of ridiculous stuff that is so far from the truth that there is no truth any more about the actual process. This is all because it suits their needs for what ever situation their movie script calls for, and no one who will be watching the final movie knows enough about hypnosis to question it's possibilities of reality.

Any psychologist with a hypnotherapy certification or certified clinical hypnotherapist would invariably laugh themselves silly or become greatly irritated at the stupidity that goes on when Hollywood tries to bring Hypnosis into the movie script. It all comes under the umbrella of PAZZAZ, combined with the public's ignorance of the process, and so far from reality it's not even close, but who knows the difference!

It's just like the guy jacking a round (bullet) into the chamber of a gun before he goes into combat, like he'd we walking around with an unloaded gun looking for the bad guys. DUH! But since most people are ignorant of guns (and Hypnosis) they don't know this so it

LOOKS/SOUNDS impressive.

Hypnosis is nothing more than your mind making reality of non-reality. When you drive down the highway and are thinking about what you've got to do when you get home, or a business deal with all the aspects involved, and you drive past your off ramp, you were in hypnosis! Your reality was somewhere else besides your conscious mind or awareness. This is what you are doing intentionally when you go into a state of hypo-relaxation. Then your SUBconscious mind is open to suggestion and those suggestions restructure what you REALLY believe about something. That belief is called your *belief system*, and it is the part that causes you to react to things in a way that you DON'T want to, if you have **poor** programming, or that you DO want to if you have **good** programming.

Essentially it's the method by which you can CHANGE your existing programming if you don't like the automatic reactions you are now exhibiting.

Like for example, when you meet someone you

are REALLY attracted to, you get nervous, fidgety, and start TRYING to be "Cool", or trying to impress them, which of course makes them start looking at their watch, needing to go to the restroom etc. You need to Reprogram these automatic responses to RELAX...let it flow, be yourself and let someone see the "Real" you. Being able to relax in the face of finally getting what you've been searching for is a tough order, but it's something you've got to learn to do. The world is full of people who when faced with getting the exact thing they've always wanted, or winning the contest they've trained for, find a way to bungle it, and some how come out a loser.

They haven't yet convinced themselves that they deserve to win, or deserve what good thing has fallen in their lap. "There must be something wrong with the world, I couldn't have possibly won", they think.

When you hear someone on the radio that was the Xth caller and won 2 tickets to go on the greatest vacation of all time, all expenses paid, they all say the same thing. "I don't believe it, you've got to be kidding, I don't believe it, are you kidding me, really!"

Their belief system has told them they are not either deserving enough, good enough, smart enough, or whatever enough to ever be this lucky. I've never heard someone say, "Wow, this is great, I knew this was going to be a great day, and I knew this was going to happen, because I'm so lucky and I deserve this!" No, I *never* heard someone say that... EVER.

What a mental reprogramming audio CD or tape does is to feed positive information into your subconscious mind in a way that it STAYS there, and changes your feeling of the way you look at events, your capabilities, what you deserve, or the way you perceive things happening around you.

There is an old Chinese saying, "*There is no right or wrong, only your perception of it.*

With that in mind, the belief system you have adopted about your ability to attract someone of the opposite sex has pretty well up to this time been set in concrete. This has been done by your personal history, as a result of past events either positive or negative.

Changing these beliefs or belief systems is next to impossible on a conscious level because of the fact that they are SUB...yes...SUBconscious. Which means if you KNOW you have them they are not SUBconscious, because you KNOW they exist, even it you try to pretend those thoughts and or beliefs are not there, or hold no value for you. THEY DO!

When you restructure your belief system to realize you can do anything you want, at any time, be with any type of people and feel comfortable with any person of your choice, then you're on your way to finding that perfect person.

Why? Because you don't NEED them.

You have realized that YOU and you alone are responsible for your own happiness, success, and also failures.

Once you realize this you begin to change things about yourself, the way you look at your accomplishments/failures. You realize that you ARE a good person, you DO have the capabilities to be successful, and now you're beginning to LIKE yourself. When you LIKE yourself, it's easy for other people (and that special person you're looking for) to like you also.

You become more relaxed, and at ease, and the feeling of "I need someone" is gone, and so is that "Needy" attitude that use to make people shy away from you. It is replaced by a self-confident (but not cocky) attitude that causes people to enjoy being around you, and acts like a magnet in attracting that special person TO you, instead of you doing all the looking & searching.

There's a lot to be said for a relaxed, mellow attitude for causing people to be attracted TO you, it's non-threatening, and it tends to make other people relax also.

That's why people will have a few drinks when they go out in a singles environment, it helps them relax. Then they think if a small amount is good, a larger amount is better and now they're drunk and TOO relaxed, and there's this police officer standing at the window of their car asking way too many questions.

Hypnotherapy is a wonderful way of *legally* teaching you how to relax in the face of pressure situations, (instead of alcohol) like wanting to look good, sound good, appear relaxed etc, making PERMINANT changes in your belief systems and gaining self-confidence is just one of them. On the next few pages are some instructions, and pointers on how to create this recording, when listened to on a once-a-day basis for about 2 weeks, WILL make a difference in your belief system, and change the way you perceive the world around you. You just have to remember to LISTEN to it!

Right now some of you are probably thinking that this is WAY too much work, and way too much effort. Someone told you this type of thing is all hogwash, and a host of other negative things that if you believe them will get you out of having to do all this work, without feeling guiltily that you're not doing enough to change your situation.

THAT'S why your "Situation" exists in it's present state...whatever that is.

Everyone has their own definition of how much "Too much" work is. It's usually based on the level of, and type of rewards derived from the amount, level, and type of work to be performed.

For the person with nothing, living under a bridge in a cardboard box, their definition of too much work is ZERO. That's whey they're there, and have accomplished ZERO!

For the guy who was cleaning windshields on the street with paper towels all day, and now owns a car wash...he didn't HAVE a definition of too much work.

The U.S. Marines have a saying, "The difficult tasks we do immediately, the impossible takes a little longer." Their definition of "Too much work", does not exist.

Remember: *NOTHING IS AS DIFFICULT OR AS EASY TO ACCOMPLISH THE **SECOND** TIME YOU LOOK AT IT.*

Don't ask why...**JUST DO IT!**

MAKING YOUR OWN REPROGRAMMING RECORDING

(Re-cap of earlier chapter)

1. Purchase a small handheld digital recorder from an audio appliance store.

2. Find a quiet place or environment where there will be no interruptions or noise.

Allow yourself to relax, and just read the following script into the recorder. If you make a mistake, stop, rewind and start over.

The INDUCTION:

Every relaxation reprogramming script has the induction portion that puts you into the relaxed state of consciousness making your subconscious open to suggestion and reprogramming. This is the set of beginning instructions for the listener to follow to achieve a mental relaxed state necessary to open the deeper part of your mental state called the subconscious mind. It is your subconscious in which we want to implant the new programming information that will bring about the outward behavior actions and reactions you desire.

For each person the time it takes for the positive reprogramming to have an outward effect, is different. For some people it happens over night, and others it takes from 3 to 15 days sometimes even longer, but one of the best things it does for you, is to teach you how to relax, and let all the tension drain out of your body, and mind. When you come back to your normal awareness you WILL feel rejuvenated, refreshed and super charged with a wonderful new energy and positive awareness.

NOTE: What you are creating here are commands for the subconscious mind to restructure your belief system. Therefore if you want to become relaxed use a "Relaxing" tone to your voice, draw out the word

R E L A X…letting your voice drop and go softer at the end. Let your voice drop at the end of the sentence or word. The opposite is true, as in the awaking; put energy into your voice to instill energy in the listener (you) so you truly awaken with a new power and energy.

THE AWAKENING

This is the part at the end of the session that

brings the listener (you) back to their normal state of awareness. In this instance you will be adding energy and also volume to your voice as you get close to the final awakening response.

SUBCONSCIOUS REPOGRAMMING SCRIPT

"ATTRACTING THE PERFECT PERSON"

INDUCTION:

GENERAL INDUCTION SCRIPT TO BE READ INTO RECORDING DEVICE OR CD BURNER

NOTE: What you are creating here are commands for the subconscious mind to restructure your belief system. Therefore if you want to become relaxed use a "Relaxing" tone to your voice, draw out the word R E L A X...letting your voice drop and go softer at the end. Let your voice drop at the end of the sentence or word. The opposite is true, as in the awaking; put energy into your voice to instill energy in the listener (you) so you truly awaken with a new power and energy.

Don't forget to actually SAY the phrase "Number xx" as you go down the script. When you see three dots ... that means to pause just a little in that spot, especially if words are repeated like,

DEEP........DEEP..... RELAXATION.

What you are trying to accomplish here is to put the listener (you) in relaxed state of mental awareness, by speaking in a slower, (as you go along) more relaxed manner, and the slower you begin to talk, and the softer you begin to talk, the more the listener (which is you) begins to relax along with the tempo of the words being spoken. Soon you will be able to go into that wonderful relaxed state much faster, much easier, and come out much more, energized and refreshed.

GENERAL INDUCTION SCRIPT

NOW I WANT YOU TO LAY BACK AND MAKE YOURSELF AS COMFORTABLE AS POSSIBLE, IN WHATEVER CHAIR, COUCH OR RECLINER YOU HAVE AVAILABLE. - I WANT YOU TO TAKE 3 DEEP BREATHS WITH ME AS I DO SO. NUMBER ONE (BREATHE IN SLOWLY...AND OUT SO THE RECORDER CAPTURES THE SOUND) NUMBER 2 (REPEAT)...NUMBER 3 (REPEAT)

NOW YOU BEGIN TO FEEL A

WONDERFUL NEW RELAXING POWER COMING OVER YOU STARTING A THE TOP OF YOUR HEAD, JUST DRAINING DOWN OVER YOUR FOREHEAD AS IT GOES, JUST RELAXING YOUR FOREHEAD CAUSING YOU TO GO LOOSE...AND LIMP

I AM GOING TO COUNT BACKWARD FROM 10 DOWN TO 1 AND WHEN I REACH 1 YOU'RE GOING TO BE IN A WONDERFUL NEW DEEP...DEEP STATE OF AWARENESS TOTALLY RELAXED AND SO AT EASE FEELING VERY COMFORTABLE, AND RELAXED

NUMBER 10...YOUR FOREHEAD BECOMES LOOSE...AND LIMP...AND THE SKIN ON YOUR FORHEAD IS COMPLETELY SLACK AND LOOSE...AND LIMP. YOU KNOW IF YOUR FORHEAD IS RELAXED YOUR ENTIRE BODY IS RELAXED AND SO YOUR FORHEAD GOES LOOSE...AND LIMP...AND YOU ARE SO DROWSEY AND ARE BECOMING MORE RELAXED THE LONGER YOU LISTEN TO THE SOUND OF MY VOICE.

NUMBER 9 – THIS MAGICAL NEW RELAXING POWER IS NOW COMING OVER YOUR NECK A SHOULDER

MUSCELS, JUST R-E-L-A-X-I-N-G YOUR NECK AND SHOULDER MUSCELS AS IT MOVES DOWN YOUR BODY

NUMBER 8 – THIS WONERFUL WARM BLANKET OF R-E-L-A-X-A-T-I-O-N (DRAW IT OUT) IS NOW MOVING INTO YOUR UPPER ARMS AND BICEPS BRINGING DEEP RELAXATION TO YOUR UPPER ARMS AND YOU GO DEEPER AND DEEPER INTO THIS WONDERFUL STATE OF DROWSEY RELAXATION

NUMBER 7 – NOW THIS POWERFUL WARM RELAXING POWER IS MOVING DOWN INTO YOUR LOWER ARMS AND YOUR FOREARMS BECOME SO LOOSE AND LIMP...AND YOU GO DEEPER DOWN INTO THIS WONDERFUL STATE OF DEEP...DEEP...R-E-L-A-X-A-T-I-O-N.

NUMBER 6 – THIS DEEP REALAXING POWER IS NOW MOVING IN TO YOUR CHEST MUSCELS CAUSING YOU TO DRIFT DOWN DEEPER AND MORE RELAXED

NUMBER 5 – YOU FEEL THIS RELAXING POWER MOVING ACROSS THE BROAD MUSCELS OF YOUR BACK TAKING ALL THE TENSION AS IT GOES

AND THESE MUSCELS GO LOOSE AND LIMP, YOU NOW FEEL SO AT EASE AND EVERY SOUND YOU HEAR MAKES YOU GO DEEPER AND DEEPER IN THE DROWSY STATE OF DEEP...DEEP...R-E-L-A-X-A-T-I-O-N

EACH AND EVERY TIME YOU LISTEN TO THESE WORDS YOU WILL GO DEEPER AND DEEPER, AND MORE RELAXED FASTER THAT THE TIME BEFORE.

NUMBER 4 – YOU FEEL THE RELAXING POWER NOW COMING IN YOUR STOMACH CAUSING YOU TO BECOME TOTALLY AT EASE MORE RELAXED THAN YOU'VE EVER BEEN...YOU GO DEEPER AND DEEPER

NUMBER 3 – THIS WARM BLANKET OF DEEP RELAXATION IS NOW MOVING INTO YOUR HANDS TOTALLY RELAXING YOUR HANDS AND ALL OF YOUR FINGERS

NUMBER 2 YOU FEEL THIS SAME WONDERFUL POWER MOVING DOWN IN TO YOUR LEGS, FIRST YOUR UPPER LEGS THEN YOUR LOWER LEGS AND CALVES TAKING ALL THE TENSION AS IT GOES, AND YOU GO DEEPER AND

DEEPER IN DROWSY DEEP RELAXATION

ON THE NEXT COUNT YOU WILL BE THERE, IN THE DEEPEST STATE OF WONDERFUL RELAXATION YOU'VE EVER BEEN, TOTALLY AT PEACE, TOTALLY AT EASE AND YOU REALIZE YOU CAN COME OUT OF THIS WONDERFUL STATE OF DEEP RELAXATION ANY TIME YOU WISH FEELING REFRESHED AND ENERGIZED, BUT NOW YOU CHOOSE TO GO DEEPER AND MORE RELAXED THAT YOU'VE EVER BEEN
EACH TIME I LISTEN TO THIS CD I GO FAR DEEPER MUCH FASTER AND I LOVE THIS FEELING OF DEEP RELAXATION, THIS IS MY REALITY COMMUNICATED TO ALL MY LEVELS.

NUMBER 1 – YOU'RE FINALLY THERE, TOTALLY RELAXED, TOTALLY AT EASE AND FEELING CENTERED AND CALM, NOW YOU WILL REMEMBER EVERY THING THAT HAS HAPPENED IN THIS SESSION AND ALLOW IT TO BE COMMITTED TO YOUR DEEPEST LEVEL OF BEING TO BE RELAYED TO ALL YOUR LEVELS OF

AWARENESS.

DEEPENING SCRIPT (This takes the listener even deeper adding to the effectiveness of the session and is very necessary to a very successful reprogramming session. You can skip it if you want but I recommend including it for total success.

NOW YOU ARE VERY DEEP IN THIS WONDERFUL D R O W S E Y STATE OF RELAXATION...BUT YOU'RE GOING TO GO EVEN DEEPER AND MMMMOOORRREEE RELAXED.

I'M GOING TO COUNT FROM 5 DOWN TO 1 AND WHEN I REACH ONE YOU'RE GOING TO BE IN A NEW WONDERFUL STATE...DEEPER....DROWSEY...DEEP RELAXATION.

NUMBER 5: FEEL YOURSELF LETTING GO EVEN MORE AND DRIFTING DOWN AS IF YOU'RE ON A WHITE FLUFFY CLOUD THAT IS LETTING COME SLOWLY TO THE GROUND

NUMBER 4 YOU ARE NOW DEEPER THAN YOU'VE EVER BEEN IN SLEEP, AND YOU ARE ENJOYING THIS DEEP FEELING OF RELAXATION EVEN MORE AND MORE.

NUMBER 3 AS YOU HEAR MY WORDS GET SLOWER AND S L O W E R AND

S L O W E R SO DO YOU GO DEEPER AND DEEPER IN THIS WONDERFUL DEEP STATE OF RELAXATION.

NUMBER 2 AS YOU HEAR MY WORDS GET SOFTER AND SOFTER...SO DO YOU GO DEEPER AND....DEEPER IN THIS WONDERFUL STATE OF DEEP RELAXATION. (Speech getting softer all the time to fade totally silent)

NUMBER 1 THERE...YOU'RE FINALLY THERE ...IN THIS NEW WONDERFUL DEEP...DEEP...STATE OF DROWSEY DEEP...RELAXATION. EACH SOUND YOU HEAR MAKES YOU GO DEEPER AND DEEPER DOWN IS THIS WONDERFUL DEEP RELAXATION.

NOW I AM GOING TO GIVE YOU SOME INSTRUCTIONS THAT WILL BE COMMITTED DIRECTLY TO THE DEEPEST PART OF YOUR MIND AND BODY, AND THESE SUGGESTIONS WILL BE CARRIED OUT AND COMITTED TO EVERY LEVEL OF YOUR BEING.

REPROGRAMMING PORTION

NOW AS YOU GO EVEN DEEPER IN THIS WONDERFUL STATE OF RELAXATION YOU ARE AWARE OF POWER THAT YOU HAVE ALSWAYS HAD THAT IS BECOMING STRONGER AND STRONGER, AND YOU ARE DEVELOPING THIS POWER TO EVEN GREATER HEIGHTS AND GREATER LIMITS THAT YOU EVER IMAGINED.

THIS IS THE POWER TO ATTRACT NEW FRIENDS AND ESPECIALLY MEN/WOMEN *(CHOOSE ONE)* THAT I FEEL WOULD FIT MY PERSONALITY, WANTS AND DESIRES.

IT IS EASY FOR ME TO MEET NEW PEOPLE AND MAKE ACCURATE EVALUATIONS OF THEIR CREDIBILITY,

PERSONALITY, AND CHARACTARISTICS.

MEN/WOMEN (PICK ONE) LIKE ME, THEY ENJOY BEING AROUND ME, AND I ENJOY THEIR COMPANY ALSO. IT IS EASY FOR ME TO ATTRACT A HIGHER LEVEL OF MEN/WOMEN EACH TIME I GO OUT IN PUBLIC, AND I BECOME BETTER AND BETTER AT COMMUINICATION WITH THESE MEN/WOMEN.

I AM A VERY GOOD LISTENER, AND I TAKE IN ALL THE INFORMATION THEY GIVE ME EASILY AND REMEMBER ALL OF THIS INFORMATION LIKE A TAPE RECORDER. I CAN RECALL THIS INFORMATION VERY QUICKLY AND THIS IMPRESSES MY NEW FRIENDS.

I HAVE A GREAT MEMORY FOR NAMES

I HAVE A GREAT MEMORY FOR NAMES

THIS IS MY REALITY COMMUNICATED TO ALL MY LEVELS

I REMEMER NAMES AND FACES VERY EASILY AND CAN RECALL THEM EASILY

AND QUICKLY.

IT IS VERY EASY FOR ME TO TELL WHEN SOMEONE IS NOT BEING TRUTHFUL WITH ME. I CAN SENSE THIS IMMEDIATELY BECAUSE OF THEIR BEHAVIOR, AND I REMEMBER IT.

THIS IS MY REALITY TO BE COMMUNICATED TO MY DEEPEST LEVEL AND TO BE RELAYED TO ALL MY LEVELS.

THESE NEW POWERS WILL REPLACE ALL OTHER REALITIES AND VIEWS ABOUT MYSELF.

I AM A WINNER IN EVERY SENSE OF THE WORD AND PEOPLE CAN TELL BY THE WAY I TALK AND LISTEN TO THEM WHEN THEY TALK.

I ENJOY MEETING NEW PEOPLE

WOMEN/MEN LIKE ME AND I ENJOY BEING AROUND THEM ALSO.

I SMILE WHEN I TALK AND THIS PUTS PEOPLE AT EASE.

THIS IS MY REALITY

I PERCEIVE LITTLE SIGNS OF ACCEPTANCE IN PEOPLE SUCH AS THE DIRECTION OF THEIR EYES.

I KNOW WHEN SOMEONE IS TELLING THE TRUTH. I AM VERY PERCEPTIVE AND PEOPLE ENJOY THIS ABOUT ME.

THIS IS MY NEW REALITY TO BE RELAYED TO ALL MY LEVELS.

NOW I AM GOING TO IMAGINE MYSELF IN A MENTAL MOVIE WHERE I WILL BE USING MY NEW FOUND POWERS OF ATTRACTION, AND PERCEPTION TO GAIN AND ATTRACT NEW FRIENDS OF THE OPPOSITE SEX.

I AM GOING TO SEE MYSELF IN SEVERAL SITUATIONS TAKING TO MEMBERS OF THE OPPOSITE SEX AND THEY ARE DEMONSTRATING BEHAVIOR THAT TELLS ME THEY LIKE ME, THAT THEY ARE COMFORTABLE IN MY PRESENCE, AND THAT THEY ENJOY MY COMPANY. WE ARE LAUGHING, AND TALKING AND MAKING

PLANS TO GET TOGETHER VERY SOON.

I WILL DO THIS NOW IN MY QUIET TIME

LET THE TAPE RUN FOR 3 MINUTES IN TOTAL QUIET, OR REMOVE THE MICROPHONE OR TURN IT OFF. THE TAPE MUST BE TOTALLY QUIET, NO SOUND WHAT SO EVER.

THERE NOW...WHAT I HAVE JUST SEEN HAS BEEN MY NEW REALITY, AND MY NEW POWER BEING DEMONSTRATED TO ATTRACT NEW MEMBERS OF THE OPPOSITIE SEX. THIS IS MY NEW REALITY AND IT IS COMMUNICATED TO MY DEEPEST LEVELS TO BE RELAYED TO ALL MY LEVELS.

AWAKENING

NOW IN A MUNITE I AM GOING TO WAKE UP AND COME BACK TO MY NORMAL STATE OF AWARENESS. I WILL REMEMBER EVERYTHING THAT HAS TRANSPIRED IN THIS RELAXTION SESSION. EACH AND EVERY TIME I LISTEN TO THIS RECORDING I GO FAR

DEEPER FAR FASTER AND I ENJOY THIS FEELING OF DEEP DEEP RELAXATION.

I AM GOING TO COUNT FROM 1 UP TO 5 AND WHEN I REACH 5 I WILL BE IN A NEW HIGHLY ENERGIZED STATE OF AWARENESS, AND POWER.

NUMBER 1 I FEEL MYSELF LETTING GO NOW OF THIS WONDERFUL DEEP STATE OF RELAXATION. I KNOW I CAN RETURN TO THIS STATE ANY TIME I WISH, BUT NOW I LET GO AND BEGIN TO COME BACK UP TO BEING WIDE AWAKE

NUBMER 2 LIKE A BUBBLE IN A GLASS OF CHAMPAIGN I AM RISING TO THE SURFACE SLOWLY RISING UP

NUMBER 3 I AM BEGINNING TO FEEL A NEW POWER AND ENERGY COURSING THROUGH MY VEINS AND MY BLOOD FEELS DE-TOXIFIED SUPERCHARGED WITH A NEW ENERGY AND ELECTRICITY.

NUMBER 4 MY EYES FEEL LIKE THEY HAVE BEEN BATHED IN COOL SPRING WATER, AND IT GIVES ME A BOOST OF

ENERGY AND CONFIDENCE THAT I ENJOY AND RETAIN WITHIN MY BODY.

NUMBER 5 WIDE AWAKE! **(CLAP HANDS)** WIDE AWAKE! I AM NOW WIDE AWAKE AND SUPERCHARGED WITH A NEW POWER AND ENERGY THAT WILL CARRY ME THROUGH REST OF THE DAY OR EVENING FOR THE NEXT 8 HOURS.

I HAVE A NEW WONDERFUL FEELING OF CONFIDENCE THAT RADIATES FROM MY BEING THAT EVERYONE AROUND ME CAN SENSE AND ENJOY.

THIS IS MY NEW REALITY TO BE COMMUNITATED TO ALL MY LEVELS AND TO BE ENJOYED CONTINUEALLY.

WAKE UP...WIDE AWAKE AND ENERGIZED!!

USE OF AUDIO HYPNOTHERAPY TAPES AND CDs

#1 RULE: NEVER...EVER PLAY IN A MOVING VEHICLE-**DRIVING OR NOT**.

#2 RULE: LISTEN IN A QUIET SECLUDED

ENVIRONMENT WITHOUT INTURPTIONS

#3 RULE: SCHEDULE PLENTY OF TIME TO LISTEN AND FULLY AWAKEN FROM THE DEEP RELAXATION

#4 RULE: IF THE RECORDINGS HELP YOU, PASS THEM ON TO SOMEONE ELSE WHO YOU THINK WILL LISTEN TO THEM.

#5 RULE: **JUST DO IT!**

CAUTION: ALWAYS ALLOW YOURSELF TO FULLY AWAKEN FROM DEEP RELAXTION THERAPY BEFORE DIRVING, OPERATING MACHINERY, USING SHARP CUTTING TOOLS OR DOING ANYTHING WHERE A HIGH DEGREE OF RESPONSIBILITY IS REQUIRED. YOU SAFETY IS OF GREAT IMPORTANCE, LIFE IS NOT A VIDEO TAPE, THERE IS NO REWIND, NO REPLAY! JUST DO IT

(AND THE BEST OF LUCK!)

About the Author
Roger W. Breterntiz
Salesman, Author, Musician, Lecturer, Trainer

A graduate of Illinois State University with a degree in Education and Southern Illinois University with a degree in design and graphics, he makes his home in Laguna Niguel, California. With certifications in clinical hypnotherapy and Neuro Linguistic Programming he is currently presenting lectures and seminars on the art of successful interaction with the opposite sex and quality communication necessary to make it happen. As manager of the Los Angeles office of a prominent singles organization for 20 years, he has the distinction of introducing hundreds of singles that resulted in becoming engaged or married within that time period. Many of the truths and directives in this book have come from the hundreds of focused first hand observations, and interaction of single people in a host of different spontaneous situations and events. Hopefully you can learn from some of these without having to experience first hand the negative part of making the same wrong choices and or choosing the wrong partner for too long a period of time.

The best of luck in your quest to find that perfect person to complement the rest of your life, and never forget the winner's creed, *"JUST DO IT!"*

Thanks for your interest,
Roger W. Breternitz CCht.
Web site: http://www.awinnersway.com

OTHER POWERFUL STUFF YOU MIGHT NEED

ON AMAZON .COM

Winning, It's a Lot More Fun! By Roger W. Breterntiz CCht. Copyright 2012 – Vector Studios

Winning at Sales, It's a Lot More Money! By Roger W. Breterntiz CCht.
Copyright 2013 - Vector Studios

Harry the 60 Pound Guard Cat - By Roger W. Breternitz
Copyright 2011 - Vector Studios

Web site: http://www.awinnersway.com Hypnotherapy self-improvement & behavior modification CDs on a variety of subjects such as:

- Quit Smoking & Weight Loss
- Don't Drink & Drive
- Insomnia
- Stress Management
- Championship tennis
- Championship Trapshooting
- Championship Archery
- Custom CDs made for specific problems

www.ingramcontent.com/pod-product-compliance
Lightning Source LLC
Chambersburg PA
CBHW061631040426
42446CB00010B/1363